THE
INDEPENDENTS IN THE
ENGLISH CIVIL WAR

'...the godly gang...'

CLEMENT WALKER

'Independency is the only lint that can stanch our wounds, the only dam that can stay the inundation of blood, which is else likely to overwhelm us.'

JOHN GOODWIN

Ge.1428

THE
INDEPENDENTS IN THE
ENGLISH CIVIL WAR

BY

GEORGE YULE

CAMBRIDGE
AT THE UNIVERSITY PRESS

MELBOURNE UNIVERSITY PRESS

1958

PUBLISHED BY
THE SYNDICS OF THE CAMBRIDGE UNIVERSITY PRESS

Bentley House, 200 Euston Road, London, N.W.1
American Branch: 32 East 57th Street, New York 22, N.Y.

AND

MELBOURNE UNIVERSITY PRESS

Carlton N. 3, Victoria, Australia

©

MELBOURNE UNIVERSITY PRESS

1958

Printed in Great Britain at the University Press, Cambridge
(Brooke Crutchley, University Printer)

PREFACE

THE problems raised in this book had been occupying the author's attention for some time, but because of the lack of source material in Australia, little could be done towards their solution.

Through the generosity of the Rockefeller Foundation, enabling research at Oxford, some at least of the problems were resolved and many others raised and left unsolved in the process.

My thanks are due to Professor R. H. Tawney who has guided my researches almost from their inception, and who has taken endless pains to read over all my early drafts; Mr Christopher Hill and Mr Trevor-Roper at Oxford were most helpful in their suggestions and criticisms, and drew my attention to many sources. Dr Geoffrey Nuttall, Lecturer in History at the Congregational Church College in London, put his learning on the history of seventeenth-century Puritanism at my service. His excellent work, *Visible Saints—The Congregational Way 1640–1660*, which appeared while this book was in proof, adds much to our knowledge of the extent of Independency. Mr Donald Pennington of the University of Manchester gave me much information and his book, *Members of the Long Parliament*, has saved me from many errors.

Dr W. G. Hoskins, Mr J. P. Cooper, Mr L. Stone and Mrs V. I. Pearl of Oxford; Dr C. M. Williams of Melbourne; Dr Carruthers of London and Mr John MacCormack of the Institute of Historical Research all gave much valuable information; and Professor R. M. Crawford, Associate-Professor Kathleen Fitzpatrick and Rev. Arthur Burns of the University of Melbourne have helped me with their interest and encouragement.

My special thanks are due to Miss M. K. Scott and Miss B. M. Ramsden of the Melbourne University Press who spent much time on the manuscript and the proofs, and to my wife, who also typed and re-typed the manuscript and gave much valuable criticism.

G.Y.

UNIVERSITY OF MELBOURNE

CONTENTS

Contents

INTRODUCTION

THE English Civil War still remains something of an enigma. Many careful studies have been made of various aspects, and bold interpretations offered of the whole, yet the puzzle is not fully solved. Why did the war break out? Why did the opposing parties find supporters?

The bold interpreters have found the mainspring to be religion, political or legal theory, economic or class interest. The careful students of detail have sorted out various pieces of the jig-saw, but the very clarity of small sections has often made the perspective of the picture more difficult to discover.

The chief difficulty, I believe, is to correlate the religious motive with the social and political. With the exception of work on the Levellers, no attempt has been made to clear up this difficult problem, and unfortunately the excellent work done on this movement has tended to give it a pre-eminence in recent interpretations at the expense of certain more important factors in the war. Because the Levellers appeared to fit so neatly into a certain pattern of classes, this pattern was then extended to include all the contestants of the conflict in an arbitrary fashion, with insufficient supporting evidence. The same care that has been given to the study of the Levellers must also be spent in examination of the other parties.

This essay is an attempt to discover the connexion between the Parliamentary Independent party and religious Independency. The old Whig interpretation of the Civil War made a simple equation between the political Independents and all those who desired religious toleration. This view does not square with either the religious or political facts, for as the events of 1647–60 show, the Independents were not a homogeneous party. On the other hand, there was a connexion, strong though undefined. In the early seventeenth century, men were insistent on precision in theological matters, and terms such as Independent or Presbyterian, even when used in a loose, popular way, had some connexion with their strict definition.

In the seventeenth century religion rather than politics or economics was the medium of thinking through which men viewed the world. This does not mean that they were better or more religious men. But it does mean that religious categories were regarded as more important than they are nowadays, although today we have our power-crazed 'priest-kings' who create religious mythologies out of their state systems, and we have some democratic leaders who attempt to use Christianity for political ends to combat them. Both these forms of idolatry were unnecessary in the seventeenth century when, except for a few persecuted Separatists, men assumed that Church and State were so bound together that social theory was a branch of theology, as set out in the work of Aquinas or Calvin. Consequently the label Independent is likely to mean something, revealing the type of society desired by men of that religious persuasion, whether they were deeply religious or merely self-deceived. Worldly men, too, who wanted a particular type of society might see in Independency the best theological expression for this society. This might well be the case for some of the Republicans of the period.

It has been assumed that the problem of the Independents had a simple religious explanation. Incited by the political and religious tyranny of Charles I's regime, all Puritans united in overthrowing him by force. In the hour of victory, the Puritans divided among themselves. The Presbyterians demanded the setting-up of a strong religious discipline; the Independents insisted on religious toleration, and this basic division led to conflict so bitter that many Presbyterians even joined the Royalist party.

This straightforward explanation seemed to fit the facts. Then in 1938 Professor Hexter published an article in the *American Historical Review* in which he claimed that the majority of the Independent members of Parliament were Presbyterian elders. This of course completely upset the theory, although years before W. A. Shaw had shown that the Presbyterians of the Long Parliament were not real Presbyterians, which should have made later writers hesitate before giving so simple an analysis. Hexter's article is one of the very few, if not the only one, to deal with this problem of the Independent political party, and will be examined in detail

Introduction

with the aid of evidence that leads me to a radically different interpretation.

The result of his work was that the religious factor tended to be ignored in discussions on the subject and that historians were satisfied to attempt purely sociological interpretations. Mr Maurice Dobb put forward the interesting, but (I believe), incorrect suggestion that the Independents represented the newer merchant class in opposition to the older medieval type of merchants.[1] Mr Trevor-Roper in a fascinating study[2] considers that the Independents represented the lesser and declining gentry, who had invariably been excluded from the lucrative and socially important government and court offices. My opinion is that this theory, which, if correct, would explain so much, unfortunately needs certain modifications which rob it of some of its explanatory value. Nevertheless, it remains the most scholarly attempt to solve this problem.

Why was the political group called 'Independent'? Why was a religious term used to designate the party? Labels always mean something, even though they may lose their original meaning. Nowadays for a variety of reasons we like to keep our political, economic and social life away from religious 'interference', or our religion away from political, economic or social 'contamination', so that we find difficulty in thinking of religion as permeating the whole of life. For the men of the seventeenth century, religious categories were always important, even for the most irreligious, and in trivial affairs. But politics were not trivial, and a large percentage of the Long Parliament was far from irreligious. Therefore it seems that there is some real religious significance in the otherwise strange coincidence that the Independent political party was named after a church, even though it might have been for many a cloak, conscious or unconscious, of many worldly motives.

In view of this apparent lack in sociological interpretations, I have tried to find out the theology of Independency, and to see whether these doctrines have any social significance. Granted that they have a theological significance in their own right, and as such are

[1] *Studies in the Development of Capitalism*, pp. 169ff.
[2] 'The Gentry, 1540–1640', *Economic History Review* Supplement (1953).

I-2

important in the history and life of the Church, nevertheless, under original sin and the ambivalence of human nature, theological reasons will not be the only motives for the adoption of these doctrines. All manner of personal prejudice and class interest may play a part—and sometimes a determining part. The Levellers, almost to a man, were Separatists in their doctrine of the Church. What were the Independents? The theological distinction between the Independents and the mass of the Puritan sects has been well known to a few Church historians, but the difference has rarely been noted by students of political and social history, and never, to my knowledge, has the significance of this distinction been discussed, except in an outstanding book by A. S. P. Woodhouse, *Puritanism and Liberty*. When we fully understand the connexion between religion and politics in the seventeenth century, one of the major problems of the Civil War will have been solved.

CHAPTER I

The Religious Origins of the Independents

EARLY PURITANISM

IT is not easy to set out what precisely the Independents as a group desired, even in the religious sphere. It is generally assumed that they were the party of toleration, but many who advocated toleration were not Independents, while in New England, 'that happy bishopless Eden' of Independency, toleration was far from conspicuous. Some light is found in the history of Puritanism.

The roots of Puritanism are probably deeper in English history than it is possible to trace. The fact that it flourished in the former strongholds of Lollardry is suggestive; compare, for example, the map in Trevelyan's *England in the Age of Wycliffe* with that in R. G. Usher's *Reconstruction of the English Church*.[1] Puritanism certainly drew on Lutheran and Zwinglian sources before the Marian exile. After that, however, I think it is true to say that Calvinism largely supplied its theology for a long period. The chief emphases of Calvin had been, first, on union with Christ and obedience to Christ;[2] second, on the depravity of man, which meant that no part of man's being, nor of human institutions escaped the taint of self-deception through pride and self-love;[3] and third, on the doctrine of the Church, Reformed, Catholic, embracing the whole of life and independent of State control. This was the ideal, and in almost every point it clashed with the aims of the Tudor despot whose desire for the all-embracing control of affairs was matched by her Tudor skill in disguising her methods of attaining it.

---

[1] I, 255.   [2] T. F. Torrance, *Kingdom and Church*, pp. 100-4.
[3] The doctrine of total depravity does not mean that there is no good at all in man but that every area of man's nature—his reason, his emotions, his will—is affected by 'the Fall'. Therefore he cannot gain salvation by freeing his spirit from his body as the Idealists say, nor his reason from his emotions, as the rationalists say, nor his emotions from his rationalizations, as the Romantics say, for they are all tainted with corruption.

On Elizabeth's accession, all the important posts in the Church were given to the ministers of less Calvinistic training,[1] so that the Calvinist group felt that it had to choose between staying within a partially reformed Church in the interests of catholicity, or breaking with it in the interests of reform. Most, at the instigation of Knox and Bullinger,[2] remained, attempting to reform the Church from within. This was the core of the Presbyterian party of the later Elizabethan period, which, after unsuccessful attempts to reform the Church through preaching, obtaining lectureships in key positions, pamphleteering and Parliamentary means,[3] finally attempted what was nothing less than secretly setting up a thoroughgoing Presbyterian system within the Anglican Church, while remaining within the letter of the law.[4] It was a bold policy, and in certain dioceses such as Peterborough, the classis movement was remarkably successful.[5]

However, Elizabeth could not tolerate any important sphere of life being independent of her control. Archbishop Whitgift could see clearly that this Presbyterianism 'impugned her majesty's royal prerogatives and government', especially by 'making her highness subject to the censures and excommunications of their eldership and other assemblies. For else she cannot be a child of the Church...'.[6] That was too much for the Supreme Governor of the Church in England to swallow, and she jibbed. The movement was quickly suppressed in 1592 when its leaders were arrested.

Although most Presbyterians stayed rather uneasily within the Church of England, there were others so intent on reform that to attain it they left the Church to form separate congregations which, in their opinion, were thoroughly reformed. In the dilemma confronting the Puritans, between catholicity unreformed or Separatist reformation, they chose reformation, whereas the Presbyterians had chosen catholicity.

[1] M. Knappen, *Tudor Puritanism*, pp. 171 ff.

[2] *Ibid.* pp. 205, 214.

[3] See J. E. Neale, *Elizabeth I and her Parliaments* for illuminating information on the relationship between Puritanism and Elizabeth's Parliaments.

[4] R. G. Usher, *The Presbyterian Movement* (Camden Society, 1905), p. xxii.

[5] Strype, *Annals*, II, 1, 133–40.   [6] Strype, *Whitgift*, III, 235.

The tendency for Christians to form sects in the interests of righteousness has been a continuous feature of the history of the Church. Troeltsch's distinction between church-type and sect-type Christianity, if not pressed too hard, is illuminating for the history of Puritanism, although there was hardly one Puritan group that was either pure sect-type or pure church-type, for since Calvin the two ideals had been brought very close together. By his intense system of discipline he had tried to give the reformed Church the close-knit unity found in the sect.

In sect-type Christianity the individual withdraws from the world into the moral and religious rigour of the sect, to which only the godly are admitted. There is more stress on personal experience and moral rectitude, and much less on the objective means of grace— the sacraments and official priesthood. As the emphasis is on personal experience rather than on the permeation of society by the objective grace with which the Church is imbued, there is furthermore almost invariably a demand for the complete separation of Church and State.[1]

The first Puritan groups to break away probably did so without any theology of separation. There is reason to think that even Richard Fitz, whose congregation was committed to prison for separation in 1576, looked upon his sect as the forerunner of the whole Church,[2] while even Browne advocated separation not as an end in itself, but as a means of truly reforming the Church of England.[3] Barrowe, however, believed that complete separation was a necessary end in itself, for the Church of England was an utterly false church, whose assemblies stood 'subject to a popish and antichristian government', whose 'worship is superstitious, devised by men idolatrous, according to that patched popish Portius, their service book...'.[4] The sixteenth-century Church and State were so inextricably linked that separation from the State church would soon lead to a theology of complete separation of Church and State. Implied by Barrowe, it is explicit in Roger Williams.[5]

---

[1] E. Troeltsch, *The Social Teaching of the Christian Churches*, I, 331 ff.
[2] C. Burrage, *Early English Dissenters*, I, 80–3. [3] *Ibid*. ch. III.
[4] Quoted in B. Hanbury, *Historical Memorials of the Independents*, I, 53.
[5] See 'The Bloody Tenent of Persecution', partly reprinted in A. S. P. Woodhouse, *Puritanism and Liberty*.

Elizabeth set out to crush both branches of Puritanism. For the next fifty years most church-type Puritans were uncomfortable members of the Anglican Church, on the whole giving up the ideal of a thoroughly reformed church in the Presbyterian fashion, so that Baxter could say that in 1640 he had never heard anyone advocate it.[1] Instead, they became more and more concerned with the minutiae of personal behaviour; this is the period when the so-called Puritan ethic really developed. They attempted to remedy the abuses in the church services by buying up livings and planting Puritan ministers in as many parish churches as they could.[2]

The Separatists continued as persecuted underground minorities, but many had frequent periods of exile in Holland, which brought them in contact with continental sects whose theology was often far removed from the semi-Calvinism of the English Separatists themselves. During this period, non-Calvinist theology—Baptist, Quietist, and Chiliastic—took a strong grip on the English sects. Their theology differed, but all agreed that Church and State should be separate, and would have nothing to do with that 'synagogue of Satan' whose 'deans and prebends are the locusts mentioned in the book of Revelation'.[3]

The Elizabethan Separatists, the Brownists, are usually claimed to be the ancestors of the Independents, yet although they share many similarities, it is doubtful if such, in fact, they were. The Independents themselves repudiated a connexion.

HENRY JACOB: THE FIRST INDEPENDENT CONGREGATION

Thoughtful Puritans found an appeal in both positions, that of those remaining within the Church of England and preserving unity, and hence unity of Church and State, and that of the Separatists with their rigorous logic. Henry Jacob in 1616 tried to preserve the best in both, and set up his congregation which, while Separatist in

---

[1] 'True History of the Councils Enlarged' (1682), p. 91.
[2] E. W. Kirby, 'The Lay Feoffees', *Journal of Modern History* (1942), pp. 1 ff., and I. M. Calder, *American Historical Review*, LIII, 760 ff.
[3] Quoted in Burrage, *op. cit.* I, 205–7.

organization, nevertheless desired to remain in communion with the Church of England.[1] This, I believe, was the first Independent congregation. Jacob argued against Separation, but wanted thorough reformation. He asked permission 'to assemble together somewhat publicly to the service and worship of God', and to have his churches governed by a 'pastor, elder and deacons in our several assemblies without any tradition of men'. His congregation was willing to take the oath of supremacy and to 'keep brotherly communion with the rest of our English Churches as they are now established... and shall truly pay all payments and duties both ecclesiastical and civil'.[2] He advocated the gathering of each church under a covenant, and that each congregation within the Church of England should have the power to determine its own policy without the assistance of a bishop or even of a presbytery. Bradshaw, his associate, was even more explicit on this autonomous power of the local congregations;[3] but, although he gave no power over them to an assembly or church officer, he did give it to the civil magistrate, 'who alone upon earth hath power to punish a whole church or congregation'.[4] Thus he still did not separate Church and State. However, theirs was a difficult position to maintain without breaking from the Anglican Church, and they were attacked by the Brownist congregation of Nicholas Lee as idolators because they went to parish assemblies.[5] (This is one indication that the Independents did not originate from the Brownists.)

Jacob's position was adopted by the founders of Massachusetts, such as Henry Robinson, who at one time had been a Separatist,[6] Governor Winthrop, and Higginson, whose attitude to the Anglican Church was: 'We will not say, as the Separatists were wont to say on leaving England, "Farewell Babylon, Farewell Rome," but we will say "Farewell dear England, farewell the Church of God in England and all dear Christian friends there".'[7] In Massachusetts, the paradise of the Independents, one finds neither complete

---

[1] C. Burrage, *Early English Dissenters*, ch. XII.
[2] *Ibid.* p. 286.   [3] *Ibid.* pp. 287ff.
[4] *Ibid.* p. 288.   [5] *Ibid.* p. 314.
[6] *Ibid.* p. 291.
[7] Quoted in W. W. Sweet, *History of Religion in America*, p. 72.

separation of Church and State nor toleration. It was thoroughly
Calvinist, adopting in 1648 the Westminster Confession of Faith,
and it was fanatically intolerant, disowning the English Independents for their toleration.[1] In 1651 a Congregational church
polity was riveted on the colony under civil laws.[2]

The issue between Independency and complete Separation was
shown by Roger Williams the Separatist in his 'Bloody Tenent of
Persecution'. The Church in his ideal should be as distinct from the
civil State as say a 'company of East India or Turkey merchants
...in London' whose activities in no wise affected the peace of the
city, even though they themselves fell to pieces, 'because the
essence or being of the city...is essentially distinct from those
particular societies'.[3] As the State did not need to interfere with
them, so there must be no interference with matters of religion:
'For God requireth not a uniformity of religion to be enacted or
enforced in any civil state.' He attacked the Presbyterians and
Anglicans for confounding civil and religious spheres of life, and
then most significantly turned to survey the Independents.

This latter...jumps with the Prelates, and though not more fully, yet
more explicitly than the Presbyterians, casts down the crown of the Lord
Jesus at the feet of the civil magistrate. And although they pretend to
receive their ministry from the choice of two or three private persons in
church-covenant, yet would they fain persuade the mother, Old England,
to imitate her daughter New England's practice, viz., to keep out the
Presbyterians and only to embrace themselves both as the state's and the
people's bishops.[4]

'An Apologetical Narration', 'The Ancient Bounds', and the
Introduction to Cotton's 'Keys of the Kingdom of Heaven' were
three manifestos issued by Independents themselves. A group of
ministers who had been driven to Holland by Laud's persecution
adopted the Independent position, partly because of Robinson's
influence and partly because of their peculiar situation, with their
English-community churches in a foreign country. On returning
into the ecclesiastical wilderness of the Civil War period, they set

[1] W. K. Jordan, *The Development of Religious Toleration*, III, 350.
[2] *Ibid.*   [3] Quoted in Woodhouse, *op. cit.* p. 297.
[4] *Ibid.* p. 287.

out these three pamphlets, and from the controversies which they engendered came the general lines of Independent thought. These remained fairly consistent and influenced some political Independents, notably Ireton.

In these pamphlets they disclaimed Separatism. Theirs was 'that very middle-way...between that which is called Brownism and the Presbyterial government as it is practised'.[1] This was a persistent claim in Independent writings, and Baillie remarked that the Independents took it ill from any man to be called Brownists.[2] Indeed, all the knowledgeable writers of the time, such as Baxter,[3] Clarendon[4] and Baillie,[5] did in fact distinguish between Independents and Sects. Whether the Independents actually were so different from the Brownists is another matter, but the significant point was that they thought themselves to be. Indeed, a study of the Army Council Debate at Whitehall in 1648 shows that it was not just a verbal difference.

ORTHODOX INDEPENDENCY

What the Independents emphasized at first was not toleration, not new doctrine, not separation of Church and State. In their manifesto of 1643, 'The Apologetical Narration', four leading Independents, Nye, Goodwin, Burrowes and Bridge, maintained that it was 'the most abhorred maxim' that 'a single and particular society of men, professing the name of Christ, and pretending to be endowed with a power from Christ to judge them that are the same body and society within themselves, should further arrogate unto themselves an exemption from giving account to or being censurable by any other, either Christian magistrates above them or neighbour churches about them'.[6]

The aim of the Independents was a new form of Church organization, a form of decentralized Calvinism, or, as the Presbyterian

---

[1] Introduction to Cotton's 'Keys of the Kingdom of Heaven' (1644), in Woodhouse, *op. cit.* p. 296.

[2] Baillie, *Letters and Journals*, II, 299.

[3] *Reliquae Baxterianae* (1696), I, 140.   [4] *History of the Rebellion*, x, § 162.

[5] Baillie, *op. cit.* II, 299, where he indicates the Independent's dilemma.

[6] In Hanbury, *op. cit.* II, 227.

Bastwick put it, they wanted not Presbyterianism dependent but Presbyterianism independent.[1] In the small city-state of Geneva the question as to how reformed congregations should be connected did not arise, but when the reformed faith spread to the nation-state it was an important issue, and the form of organization that developed was Presbyterianism, in which local congregations were grouped under the control of presbyteries and the presbyteries were under the direction of the General Assembly in a highly organized system. The Independents placed the supreme power in the local congregation, not in presbytery or Assembly, which bodies should exist solely to give mutual help and advice. Baillie wrote:

> It hath hitherto been their earnest desire to decline the infamy of Brownism; and it was the charity of their Brethren to distinguish them from that sect, under the new name of 'Independents': importing their chief difference from us [Presbyterians] to stand not in the point of Separation, which is our proper quarrel with the Brownists, but alone in the point of church-government which, against all the Reformed Churches, they maintain to be Independent; that is, not subject to the authority and jurisdiction of any superior synod.[2]

This central Independent idea on church government was set out at the Savoy Conference of 1658, when the Independents came together to draw up a doctrinal statement. Christ, the only King and Head of the Church, calls certain people to walk together in particular societies, and 'To each of these churches...He hath given all that power and authority which is in any way needful for the carrying on that order in worship and discipline....Besides these particular churches, there is not instituted by Christ any church more extensive or catholic'.[3]

These gathered individual congregations, where evildoers were not permitted (thus maintaining the purity of the Church) were similar to the Brownists, yet without the anarchical potentialities of Brownism. Of their 'very middle-way', Nye and Thomas Goodwin

[1] Bastwick, 'Independency not God's Ordinance' (1645), pp. 5–7.
[2] Baillie, 'Dissuasive from the Errors of Our Time', in Hanbury, *op. cit.* III, 144.
[3] Quoted in Hanbury, *op. cit.* III, 545.

said that it differed from the Brownist popular government, which 'drowns the elders' votes' in that of the people's, and from the 'presbyterial government' of several congregations which 'doth... swallow up not only the interests of the people, but even the votes of the elders of that congregation....'[1]

In other respects the theoretical doctrine of Independency was very similar to Presbyterianism, and many contemporary pamphleteers urged accommodation.[2] In all essentials, the Declaration of the Savoy Conference resembled the Westminster Confession of Faith. Even the doctrine of predestination was taken over verbatim, as indeed were most of the other clauses.

But to describe the Independency of the 1640's as simply a doctrine of decentralized Calvinism may be misleading. In Massachusetts, toleration was not the essential part of its creed; but in England, in order to make headway against official Presbyterianism, the Independents at first had to claim the right to be tolerated themselves, and their ground was the right of toleration for all Christians. They thus soon became linked up with the cause of complete toleration.[3] Within Independency itself, as each congregation was independent of a central church body, variations of doctrine had inevitably appeared. Was not John Goodwin Arminian? So the Independent leaders were really concerned about toleration for Christians, toleration within the sphere of grace (the Church). It was stated in 'The Ancient Bounds', claiming for every Christian 'his right of free yet modest judging and accepting what he holds', the main end and respect of this liberty being to 'vindicate a necessary advantage to the truth'.

I contend not for variety of opinions; I know there is but one truth. But this truth cannot be so easily brought forth without this liberty; and a general restraint, though intended but for errors, yet through the unskilfulness of men, may fall upon the truth. And better many errors of some kind suffered than one useful truth be obstructed or destroyed.[4]

[1] In Woodhouse, *op. cit.* p. 296.
[2] E.g. Harrington in 'Noah's Dove' (1645).
[3] Baillie, *Letters and Journals*, II, 326.
[4] In Woodhouse, *op. cit.* pp. 247–65. The familiar statement of this view is in Milton's *Areopagitica*.

This seems a clear enough plea for toleration, but then the writer began to make distinctions. The world is divided into the spheres of nature and grace, and so is the individual conscience.

Conscience itself, as it will not be beholden to any man for its liberty so neither is it capable of outward restraint....But the exercise or practice of conscience...is properly the object of outward restraint in question....It may well beseem a state to force men to contribute to their own and the public good or safety. And though God can have no glory by a forced religion, yet the state may have benefit by a forced service. The service of the state is outward...and is perfect as to its end without the will and conscience of that person from whom it is extorted; so is not the service of God which is inward and spiritual....[1]

A magistrate by good government can prepare the way for the Gospel to enter, by restraining men from 'gross profaneness and insolent opposition to truth'.

Thus we have committed to the magistrate the charge of the Second Table [of the Commandments] viz., materially, that is, he is not to see God dishonoured by the manifest breach thereof....[1]

This is not altogether unexpected, but the writer continued:

But is that all? No, surely. He may enter the vault even of those abominations of the First Table and ferret the devils and devil-worship out of their holes and dens, so far as nature carried the candle before him.[1]

He concluded that polytheism and atheism ought to be restrained and exploded by the Christian magistrate. In places where the Gospel has been preached, custom or education are to be taken as similar to the light of nature, and so the Christian magistrate in 'an instructed commonwealth' should not tolerate denial of the Trinity, the Resurrection, the Last Judgment, etc.

A rather difficult paragraph suggested that the magistrate should have some control over the external peace and order of the churches, as disorder is a civil thing.

For there are these two things go to religion: the thing itself and the managing of it. Though conscience is not to be forced to or from the thing, yet the manner of the practice is to be regulated according to peace and comeliness by the civil magistrate.[1]

[1] Woodhouse, *op. cit.* pp. 247–65.

He, presumably, can draw a line between carol singing and holy rolling.

The magistrate should do all he can on behalf of the truth, without actually using force. He is to be 'a nursing father to the Church. ...He is to exercise a defensive power for religion both at home and abroad', but in all this, he must be impartial to all 'whom he judges to be the children of the truth in the main, though scabby or itchy children through some odd difference.' He must not try to decide differences between the truly religious, who are immune from the state's power. Persecution only drives men to worse errors, 'even as the Bishops' tyrannies did drive men to extremities ...of absolute separation and Anabaptism'.[1]

It is clear from 'The Ancient Bounds' that toleration was to be limited to 'genuine Christians' and there was to be no complete separation of Church and State. This continued to be the official 'Independent line', embodied in the 1658 Savoy Declaration, which in spite of its basically Calvinist theology, differed radically from the Calvinist temper, in its insistence that it was not designed to be a rigid doctrinal test, because force or constraint turns such matters 'from being Confessions of Faith, into exactions and impositions of faith'.[2] The necessary foundations were 'faith and holiness: in all other matters extra-fundamental, whether of faith or order' all Christian states and churches should be forbearing and mutually indulgent.[3] Wisely, perhaps, these 'necessary foundations of faith and holiness' were not defined.

This was a wider toleration than most of their leaders sought in the early 1640's, although they claimed that 'it hath been our constant principle'. Not, they hastened to add, that they were indifferent to truth, but even Christians in error should be borne with for Christ's sake, provided their errors were 'purely spiritual, and intrench and overthrow not civil societies'.[4]

How would the Independents organize Church-State relationships? It is difficult to say. If Cromwell had survived a little longer, we might have seen the establishment of a national Church made up of Independent congregations on the New England model. As it

[1] *Ibid.*
[2] In Hanbury, *op. cit.* III, 517. [3] *Ibid.* p. 520. [4] *Ibid.* p. 521.

was, under his rule there was a close connexion between Church and State despite the absence of a state Church. In 1657 he consented to 'The Humble Petition and Advice of the Knights, Citizens and Burgesses now assembled in this Commonwealth'. The eleventh clause desired the 'true Protestant Christian religion' to be 'held forth and asserted for the Public Profession of these Nations' with a Confession of Faith which none be permitted to revile or reproach, and toleration to all Trinitarian Christians of good behaviour but not to popery, prelacy or 'to the countenancing of such who publish horrid blasphemies or practise or hold forth licentiousness or profaneness under the profession of Christ'.[1] All ministers and preachers agreeing to the confession were to be esteemed 'fit and capable' although they might differ in matters of worship and discipline.

There was State support and State recognition of religion, for tithes were continued and, in addition, there was State control, by means of the Triers and such acts of Parliament as the Sabbatarian Act of 28 June 1657.[2] At least 190 Independents became ministers of parish churches. Nye was rector of St Bartholomew's, Caryl of St Mary Magnus, Greenhill and Matthew Mead joint rectors of Stepney, and William Bridge was rector of Yarmouth.[3]

With the Restoration both Independents and Presbyterians were forced to become in practice thorough-going Separatists, indistinguishable from the sects in the Babylon of nonconformity, but even then, all did not give up their theories. In 1676 Philip Nye was still maintaining that the State had a duty to perform in the sphere of grace. In 'The Lawfulness of Hearing Public Ministers of the Church of England' written to smooth over the trouble between conforming and nonconforming ministers, Nye distinguished between Gospel and national churches. God had instituted both. One was from the first commandment, directed by the Light of Nature, and the other was a duty of the second commandment, and our direction in it was only from the Gospel light. The Gospel

[1] Quoted in S. R. Gardiner, *Constitutional Documents of the Puritan Revolution*, p. 454.
[2] Stoughton, *History of the English Church*, II, 200 ff.
[3] See below, p. 21.

16

church was primarily for believers; the national church was 'principally for conversion'. The magistrate had nothing to do with the former, but a definite duty to the latter, and Nye concluded that all should support the national church also, as members of the Commonwealth.[1]

THE RADICAL INDEPENDENTS

The position outlined above was that of the classical Independents, but all Independents were not adherents to this classical model. Many, particularly in the Army, were more concerned with some implications of this dogma of decentralized Calvinism than with the dogma itself. Edwards reported 'a godly minister' as saying that the Army:

were not so much against Presbyterial Government, though many thought them so, as against being tied to any Church Government at all: for if the Parliament would set up the Independent Government, and enjoin that upon them, they should be as much against that....they held liberty of conscience; that no man should be bound or tied to any thing...that was the judgment or true genius of that sort of men in the Army, called 'Independents'.[2]

In 'What the Independents Would Have' the lawyer John Cook was obviously concerned with religious toleration not church organization, though he specifically stated that unlike the Separatists, he did not advocate toleration 'for errors against religion or the state policy'.

Cromwell, the Independent *par excellence*, was certainly not, prior to 1654 at any rate, a classical Independent. He was pre-eminently concerned with godliness and religious experience. As these were the only true marks of religion for him, he would tolerate all with these marks, whatever their church organization. He wrote from the Army in 1645:

Presbyterians, Independents, all had here the same spirit of faith and prayer...pity it is that it should be otherwise anywhere. All that believe have the real unity which is most glorious, because inward and spiritual in

[1] D. Nobbs, 'Philip Nye on Church and State', *Cambridge Historical Journal* (1935).
[2] Quoted in Hanbury, *op. cit.* III, 187.

the body and to the head. As for being united in forms, commonly called uniformity, every Christian will for peace-sake study and do as far as conscience will permit: and from brethren, in things of the mind we look for no compulsion, but that of light and reason.[1]

Coupled with the emphasis on toleration and experiential religion was the demand that the laity be permitted to preach. All filled with the spirit should have this right, demanded by most of the sects, exercised in Cromwell's Army, stated by John Cook and fought for in Parliament. This second strand in religious Independency is almost identical with thorough-going sect-type Christianity. When the debate was purely on the religious level Cromwell spoke the language of religious enthusiasm like any sectary.

But the majority of the sectaries drew radical social and political inferences from their beliefs which were not acceptable to the Independent gentry. Consequently the enthusiast Independents limited toleration to what they defined as the truly religious sphere, and joined with the classical Independents in maintaining some Church-State connexion and preserving the social cement of the parish system. Classical Independency was the most promising form of Christianity for encouraging religious enthusiasm while preserving the social framework.

It was always, of course, a most difficult position to maintain, and the dilemma was revealed as time went on. The Independents were unable to define where they stood on the crucial issue of Separatism in practice. Baillie illuminated their 'middle position' and their difficulty in maintaining it when he wrote in July 1645:

We hope shortly to get the Independents put to it to declare themselves either to be for the rest of the Sectaries, or against them. If they declare against them, they will be but a small inconsiderable company; if for them, all honest men will cry out upon them for separating from all the Reformed Churches to join with Anabaptists and Libertines.[2]

As they did not form a homogeneous group, the Independents 'could not agree among themselves'[3] on this issue, with all its related problems (such as tithes). Some, like Ireton, took the stand

---

[1] *Writings and Speeches of Oliver Cromwell*, ed. Abbott, I, 377.
[2] Baillie, *Letters and Journals*, II, 299.   [3] *Ibid.* p. 306.

of classical Independency, others, like Whitelocke, were more conservative. Some, like Cromwell, were religious enthusiasts; though, unlike most of them, that great muddled pragmatist was also socially conservative.

On the whole, the religiously radical Independents were more likely to become politically radical, while those conservative in religion remained conservative politically. Almost all Independents tended to be socially conservative. If they had been social radicals they would simply have adopted a thorough-going Separatist position like the Levellers.

CHAPTER II

The Extent of Independency

HOW widespread was Independency in the Civil War period? The evidence is uneven, and by its very nature scanty. Later, I argue that many Independents remained Presbyterians until after 1649 because they thought the parish church system was essential for the well-being of their society, so that as long as Presbyterianism was the established Church, the fact that a man was a Presbyterian elder before 1650 does not mean that he was not Independent by inclination.[1] After 1650 the situation was so fluid that only in a relatively few cases can one be certain of the religious affiliations of any one person. Even after 1640 the terms Independent, Presbyterian and to some extent Anglican, did not have the precision in practice that they had in theory. Strictly speaking, it would be hard indeed to prove that Cromwell and Vane were Independents, and it is quite certain that the great majority of the Presbyterians in the House of Commons were not genuine Presbyterians. In this period of instability, men's religious opinions did not remain static. Sir Gilbert Pickering, for example, was first an Anglican, then a Presbyterian, then an Independent, then a Sectary.[2] Many Quakers were originally Independents or Presbyterians. Presbyterians such as Rigby later became Independents.[3] Even Isaac Pennington, a leading Independent layman, was first a Presbyterian.[4] Whalley was called a Presbyterian, but Baxter, who talked with him, stated that he differed from them on a number of fundamental points.[5] And to what denomination did Baxter himself belong?

Judging by the success of the voluntary Worcestershire Association set up by Baxter in 1653 there must have been a large number

[1] See my discussion of Hexter's lists of elders, below, pp. 37–41.
[2] *D.N.B.*   [3] J. Vicars, *Dagon Demolished* (1660).
[4] E. Freshfield, *Some Remarks on the Records of St Stephen's, Coleman Street*, p. 8.
[5] *Reliquae Baxterianae*, book I, part i, pp. 55–6.

of his 'mere Christians'.[1] Even among the clergy, leading Presbyterians like Marshall did not fully satisfy the Scottish tests of Presbyterianism as put forward by Baillie.[2] Officially only about 200 Independent ministers were ejected at the Restoration but F. J. Powicke argues plausibly that the number should be nearer 500.[3] After the Restoration it is even more difficult to be precise. Out in the wilderness many Presbyterians look like Independents[4] and many Independents look like thorough-going Separatists.

Probably there were many more of those whose sympathies were towards Independency than there were pure Independents, who, as I have argued, held a very narrow middle way between Presbyterianism and Separatism. Contemporaries like Sir John Harris often distinguished between 'pure' and 'mixed' Independents. Little reliance, of course, can be placed on Edwards' 'Gangraena', but the following passage is interesting:

> The Army that is so much spoken of upon all occasions in the news-books, pulpits, conferences, to be 'Independent'—though I conceive, upon good information, that upon a true muster of the whole, commanders and common soldiers, there would not be found above one in six of that way,— yet of that Army called by the Sectaries, 'Independent', and of that part of it which is truly so, I do not think there are fifty pure Independents.[5]

Speaking of the whole body he said that they were 'a contemptible party as of themselves'.

Baillie similarly suggested a relatively low figure for London in 1645, 'much within one thousand persons; men, women and all, who to this day, have put themselves in any known Congregation of that way, being reckoned'.[6] Later he said that they were growing fast,[7] but hazarded no further guess at their strength.

---

[1] *Ibid.* book III, p. 102.

[2] Baillie, *Letters and Journals*, II, 230.

[3] *Essays Catholic and Congregational*, p. 293. My own list of probable Independent ministers in Appendix C would confirm this figure.

[4] E.g. Mr John Lucas, a Presbyterian, who on his ejection preached to the Independents at Yarmouth (J. Browne, *Congregational Churches of Norfolk and Suffolk*, p. 342).

[5] In Hanbury, *Historical Memorials of the Independents*, III, 159.

[6] 'A Dissuasive from the Errors of our Time', in Hanbury, *op. cit.* III, 135.

[7] Baillie, *Letters and Journals*, II, 177.

It seems likely that these figures are near the truth, for before the outbreak of the Civil War there were only two Independent congregations in London. They were the continuation of Henry Jacob's church, which had grown so large that it divided under the leadership of Mr Jessey and Praise-God Barbon.[1] With the return of the Dissenting Brethren from Holland and others from New England[2] the numbers undoubtedly rose. At the Westminster Assembly there were about a dozen Independent ministers, though Baillie in 1644 said that there were only three Independent parish ministers in London itself.[3] However, many more were itinerant preachers or lecturers, and so Independency grew, even though its members still attended the parish churches. In one parish, protested the Lord Mayor in 1645, there were eleven private meetings[4] (though these were not necessarily Independent meetings). Sometimes, as in the case where John Goodman was vicar of St Stephen's, Coleman Street, with the conversion of a minister to Independency a powerful congregation or a large part of it would be brought over to the Independent side. Goodman organized St Stephen's on the Independent model and refused the sacraments to all who would not subscribe to the church covenant. This proved too much for the rest of the parishioners and he was forced to leave, taking his gathered congregation with him to a nearby building. However, in 1648 he was reinstated at St Stephen's.[5]

London, even under the Commonwealth and Protectorate, was predominantly Presbyterian, but after Pride's Purge it was more fashionable to be an Independent, and many more Independent churches were set up, some in parish churches, such as St Magnus under Caryl, St Bartholomew's, Exchange under Nye, St Pancras under Cockayn, and even in Westminster Abbey.[6]

[1] E. E. Cleal, *The Story of Congregationalism in Surrey*, pp. 3–6.

[2] At least sixty ministers and many important laymen came from New England after the outbreak of the Civil War (W. L. Sachse, 'The Migration of New Englanders to New England', *American Hist. Rev.* LIII, 251 ff.).

[3] Baillie, *Letters and Journals*, II, 110.

[4] 'The Humble Petition of the Lord Mayor, Aldermen and Commons of the City of London', 16 Jan. 1645–6.

[5] Freshfield, *op. cit.* pp. 8 ff.

[6] Ira Brosely, *Ministers of the Abbey Independent Church.*

But Independency before 1660 was never numerically strong. At the Savoy Conference in 1657 where the Independents set out their beliefs, 200 delegates attended, representing 120 churches.[1] At the Restoration 190 declared Independent ministers were ejected from their churches,[2] and though a higher figure would probably give a truer picture, at the most they were only about one-quarter as numerous as the Presbyterians who were ejected.

The growth of Independency in the country was patchy. In some counties, Norfolk, Suffolk, Essex, Gloucestershire and Yorkshire, Independent ministers were fairly numerous. In other counties Independency seems almost unknown prior to 1650.[3] Outside London, East Anglia was the most important centre of Independency, but even there, before 1649 there were only six Independent churches.[4] After that, they sprang up quickly, and at the Restoration thirty Independent incumbents were forced to leave their parishes.[5] This figure of course gives no indication of those gatherings not held in parish churches. These must have been numerous, for in 1672 eighty licences were applied for under the Declaration of Indulgence.[6] The parent church at Yarmouth, which took a part in founding many other East Anglian churches, had an influential position in the district despite strong Presbyterian opposition. Miles Corbet, the M.P. and Recorder of Yarmouth, was a member here, while Bridge the Independent minister was the town chaplain.[7] Norwich was even stronger after 1643 when many 'godly in Norwich expressed their desire of joining in the Church Fellowship', although in November 1645 the number was only 114.[8]

The impression gained from the scanty facts is that the strength of Independency before 1649 depended more on the influence of a leading minister, such as Bridge at Yarmouth, or Nye who was at Hull for a short time, than on the numbers of local residents who might favour it. After 1649 it was a different matter, for the

---

[1] Hanbury, *op. cit.* III, 517.

[2] G. F. Nuttall, 'Congregational Incumbents under the Commonwealth', *Congregational Historical Society Transactions*, vol. XIV.

[3] *Ibid.*

[4] J. Browne, *op. cit.* p. 164.   [5] Nuttall, *op. cit.*

[6] F. Bates, *The Declaration of Indulgence 1672*, appendix VII.

[7] J. Browne, *op. cit.* p. 458.   [8] *Ibid.* pp. 216ff.

government actively helped and protected these small groups, who often included leading members of the administration. Whitelocke, for example, belonged to George Cockayn's congregation,[1] while Robert Coke, brother of the Cromwellian judge, succeeded Bridge at Yarmouth.[2] Independency, if anything, was the established religion, and Independents could be both Independents and parish ministers. Consequently many of the gentry who favoured Independency but had previously hesitated to break from the parish church system could be now openly Independent and at the same time retain the parochial system. Now, when the patron of a church living was an Independent, he often either installed an Independent minister, or, like the Brewsters at Wrentham, made the parish church openly Independent.[3] John Lisle of Moyles Court installed the Independent John Warner at Christchurch, Hampshire.[4] At Bungay, Zephaniah Smith had been installed by 'the especial care and prudence' of the Protector, despite opposition of 'the malignant party'[5] and he received the customary tithe.[6]

There was often fierce rivalry with the Presbyterians in the towns. At Monmouth, Walter Craddock lamented:

We are the most miserable men in the world in this poor city: if a man had as much grace as Paul had, if some Independent see him and say he is inclining to Presbyterianism, or if a Presbyterian see him and say he is inclining to Independency, then let him go and cut his throat....[7]

In Nottingham too, feeling ran high[8] and the issue seems to have affected local politics at Yarmouth and Norwich.[9] At Exeter, a strong Puritan centre, whose bishop from 1627–41, Joseph Hall, had treated Puritans very leniently, the town council was strongly Independent. In 1649 the mayor dropped the proclamation of the Covenant in the gutter, and ejected Mr Ford, the Presbyterian minister, for refusing to take the oath to be loyal to the Common-

---

[1] *Congregational Hist. Soc. Trans.* (1933–5), p. 225.
[2] J. Browne, *op. cit.* pp. 252ff. [3] *Ibid.* pp. 421ff.
[4] *Congregational Hist. Soc. Trans.* VII, 280.
[5] J. Browne, *op. cit.* p. 510.
[6] W. A. Shaw, *History of the English Church during the Civil Wars*, II, 595.
[7] *Congregational Hist. Soc. Trans.* XIII, 13.
[8] *Ibid.* (1933–5), p. 103. [9] J. Browne, *op. cit.* p. 510.

wealth.[1] In 1650 the Cathedral was divided in two for the separate use of Presbyterians and Independents.[2] This expedient of division of the large parish church was not uncommon—it was made at Hull,[3] and Newcastle as well, where Presbyterians and Independents were amicable. Newcastle however was probably exceptional; a Puritan preacher of the district, Cuthbert Sydenham, wrote praising the respect he had been shown by the corporation, adding that for nine years when the rest of England had been

in a puzzle about errors, sects and schisms, even almost to blood, you have sat as in a Paradise, no disturbances in your pulpits, no railings or disputings, Presbyterians and Independents preaching in the same place, fasting and praying together in heavenly harmony...and as for the errors of the times that have disturbed so many towns in England, it may be said of Newcastle as of Ireland, the air is so pure no such venomous creature can live there.[4]

It is difficult to explain the frequent and often violent antipathy between Presbyterians and Independents within the towns. The theory that the Presbyterians were the party of London and the Independents the party of the provinces has not taken account of this fact. A simple religious explanation is, I think, unsatisfactory. The fight was never between the clergy alone. It was carried on in town councils too. The religious struggles always took some social form. What was it, and why was Newcastle exempt? We need to know more of the local histories of these towns to answer these questions.

Independency seems to have been very weak in most western counties. In Staffordshire,[5] Herefordshire, Monmouthshire, Westmorland, Somerset and Cornwall only three of the parish ministers ejected in 1660 were undoubtedly Independents, though a few others may also have been.[6] In some east-midland counties like Huntingdonshire,[7] strange to say, there were only a few Independent ministers, although this is only an indication that those who controlled the

---

[1] W. J. Harte, *Devonshire Assoc. Trans.* (1937), pp. 44 ff.
[2] *Ibid.* p. 50.
[3] *Congregational Hist. Soc. Trans.* IX, 31.
[4] *Memoirs of Ambrose Barnes* (Surtees Soc. vol. 50), p. 365.
[5] A. G. Matthews, *The Congregational Churches of Staffordshire*, p. 33.
[6] See Appendix C.   [7] *Ibid.*

livings in these counties were almost certainly not Independents (in itself, of course, *prima facie* evidence that Independency was not strong there). It was in counties such as Dorset where Presbyterianism was never seriously implemented that the churches were to all intents and purposes Independent.[1]

However one regards the evidence, it seems certain that before 1650 open Independents were a tiny minority; that after 1650 with the favour of the government and the ability to make parish churches Independent, their number increased fairly rapidly, but at the most reached only a quarter of the numerical strength of the Presbyterians.[2] How, then, did they become so very influential?

Part of the answer is obvious. This minority must have had some influential support. If my analysis of the Independent theology is correct, this is not unlikely. As it did not really separate Church and State, nor advocate a complete toleration that might endanger either institution with revolutionary opinions from Münster, Independency could, in fact, be controlled by the State more readily than could Presbyterianism, with its strong central organization. It is significant that, partly for propaganda reasons, the Independent apologists so frequently upheld the rights of the civil magistrate.

In the initial stages of the movement, special efforts were apparently made to gain influential converts. Baillie, in remarking how few they were, added: '...setting aside number, for other respects they are of so eminent a condition that not any, nor all the rest of the Sects are comparable to them'.[3] Clarendon's testimony agrees. The Independents 'had not so great congregations with the common people but were followed by the most substantial and wealthy citizens and by others of better condition. To these men Cromwell and most of the officers in the Army adhered.'[4] Edwards accused them of deliberate proselytizing among the wealthy[5] and

---

[1] W. Densham and J. Ogle, *The Story of Congregational Churches in Dorset*, p. 119.

[2] See estimate in Wolfe, *Milton and the Civil War*, pp. 66, 268. See also H. F. Saunders, 'Nottinghamshire Independency', *Congregational Hist. Soc. Trans.* (1933–5), p. 104.

[3] Baillie, 'Dissuasive', in Hanbury, *op. cit.* III, 135.

[4] Clarendon, *History of the Rebellion*, x, § 174.

[5] *Antapologia*, p. 222.

added that Nye 'having lived a great part of his time since his return into England in noblemen's families and in Yorkshire...hath played the politician the more...particularly at Hull'.[1] Bastwick described them as the wealthy dilettantes of the Puritan party. 'You shall find their houses furnished rather like noblemen and peers than ordinary men...and their fare and diet is so delicious and set out with such curiosity of cookery...as they exceed the very princes of the world.'[2]

This is hardly likely, but may be taken to indicate that the Independents were not of the same social strata as the poor 'tub preachers' and 'mechanical dippers'. Bastwick made two further observations. First, that 'their Independent itinerary preachers run from place to place'—a number of the leading Independents were, in fact, lecturers rather than settled ministers. This could partly account for the fact that many more people seemed to favour Independency than were in actual Independent congregations. If there were no Independent congregation in their locality, they had no real alternative but to attend the national Presbyterian Church or turn sectary. (For example, Sir William Brereton was a Presbyterian elder, although his inclinations were obviously Independent, for he had an Independent chaplain.[3])

Bastwick's second remark was that on the return from Holland at the outbreak of the Civil War, the Independents were given the greatest honours and 'settled in the Prime Lectures of the kingdom' and that their congregations 'consisted of great personages, knights, ladies and rich merchants' and that the poor felt ill at ease in their presence.[4] This was not a wholly true picture. Some of the Independent churches consisted of poor folk. At Bury St Edmunds there were only six members of the Independent congregation in 1654 able to give financial support.[5] (This was rather a sect-type than a parish-church type of Independency.) On the other hand, it may reflect something of the social composition of some of the

[1] *Ibid.* p. 217.
[2] 'Independency not God's Ordinance', in Hanbury, *op. cit.* III, 81.
[3] See Appendix A, p. 90.
[4] 'Independency not God's Ordinance', *loc. cit.* p. 91.
[5] J. Browne, *op. cit.* p. 395.

better known Independent congregations, for in that socially conscious age, it would be better propaganda against them to be able to represent the Independents as poor, mean and insignificant. Undoubtedly the Independents had the support of influential people, many of whom were connected with the Massachusetts Bay Company. Lord Brooke probably held Independent meetings at Warwick Castle,[1] and he and Lord Say and Sele were counted by Baillie as the only two Independent peers.[2] One of the clearest expositions of Independency is Brooke's 'Discourse on the Nature of Episcopacy', with his argument that Independent government in communion with the Church of England was the religious ideal for the colonies.[3] Later on, Lord Wharton was the great supporter of nonconformity in general and Independency in particular.[4]

But two or three peers are not whole congregations. Who in fact among the upper strata of society did support the Independents? The answer leads to the heart of the problem, the relationship between the Independent churches and the Independent political party.

[1] J. Sibree and M. Caston, *Independency in Warwickshire*, p. 125.
[2] Baillie, *Letters and Journals*, I, 275.
[3] Reprinted in Haller and Davies, *Tracts on Liberty*, vol. II.
[4] See Appendix A, p. 125.

CHAPTER III

The Independents and the Long Parliament

THE EARLY STAGES

HOW did Independency influence the political life of England during the Civil War?

When the Long Parliament first met, the Independents apparently had little, if any, effect on the situation, but then, in the early days of the conflict, a change in the personnel of the government would appear to be the only probable change that was contemplated by any of the Parliamentary leaders. The old court rulers of 'Thorough', having thrown in their hand, were replaced by a new group, men like the Earl of Bedford, who, Clarendon said, 'only intended to make himself and his friends great at court, not at all to lessen the court itself'.[1]

Even when the religious question was raised in the Root and Branch Bill, Independency was not the issue—nor, for that matter, was Presbyterianism. Hexter[2] suggests that the matter of religion that was to prove so explosive was not allowed to arise as long as Pym lived, and so did not become an issue until after his death, but this may not be an adequate account. As will be shown, a definite Independent political group, allied with Independent churchmen, was active by October 1643.

Hexter[3] shows that in the early stages of the war there were three fairly well defined groups aligned on the Parliamentary side. The peace party, with its strict constitutionalism, and eager for peace at almost any price, was prepared to rely entirely on the King to keep his word. In the war party were those who had overreached themselves, the few genuine Republicans—and, I would add, some religious enthusiasts—who would not trust the King one inch until they had the upper hand in war to enforce his word for him.

---

[1] *History of the Rebellion*, III, §§ 25, 50ff.
[2] *The Reign of King Pym*, p. 97.   [3] *Ibid.*, particularly chs. III and IV.

A middle group, controlled by Pym and Hampden, wanted peace but believed they must be prepared for war because they could not trust the King. This group of a mere thirty-five or forty members of Parliament[1] held the balance of power, and was instrumental in bringing in the Scots. This policy of reluctant war was maintained by the middle group until the death of Pym, when the power in Parliament passed to the war party.

Vane and St John came to be the new leaders of the House. They had belonged to the radical wing of the middle group, but joining forces with the war party,[2] actually controlled it, because, being radicals in religion, they wished to ensure not only total victory, but a measure of toleration against the Presbyterianism which the Scots alliance made obligatory. It was about the time of the Self-Denying Ordinance in 1644 that the term Independent came to be commonly used of this more radical party in Parliament, though it was not infrequently used the year before.

These radicals had control of Parliament. They had, through Alderman Pennington, some kind of a control in London. By the skilful chicanery of the Self-Denying Ordinance (moved by an innocent Presbyterian, Zouch Tate) the Army too was theirs. In contemporary accounts of the incident, the role of Independency was clearly seen. 'The Independent party', bemoaned Baillie, 'lying always at watch...began lustily to play their game. Their first assay was on Manchester's Army, there they had cast their strength under Cromwell. All Sectaries who pleased to be soldiers for a long time casting themselves from all the other, arrives under his command, in one body.'[3] 'This hath been the Independents' great plot by this army, to counterbalance us, to overawe the Assembly and Parliament both to their ends.'[4]

But having gained the Army, the Independents lost control of Parliament, and also, presumably, of London. The less radical members of Parliament, the remnants of the old middle party, took fright at the turn of events and sided consistently with Holles and the Presbyterian 'peace party' (Holles in his *Memoirs* noted that

[1] *The Reign of King Pym*, p. 70.
[2] Baillie, *Letters and Journals*, II, 234.
[3] *Ibid.* pp. 234–5.   [4] *Ibid.* pp. 229–30.

former radicals came over to his party). Until they used force, the Independents never again controlled Parliament,[1] which was now in the hands of the Presbyterians.

THE PRESBYTERIANS

After Queen Elizabeth had crushed the efforts of the Presbyterians in 1593, the chief concern of the Puritan movement had ceased to be with church organization and turned more to matters of morality and worship. The vast majority of Puritans were within the Church of England. The Separatist minority was formed almost entirely of poor people who were no real threat to the government. But the Puritans within the Church were. They had an organization backed by powerful laity to buy up livings and fill them with Puritan clergy, although they were not, after about 1620, primarily hoping for a new type of church framework.[2]

Baxter wrote on the common definition of Puritan:

My father never scrupled common-prayer or ceremonies, nor spake against Bishops, nor ever so much as prayed but by a Book or Form, being not even acquainted then with any that did otherwise. But only for reading Scripture when the rest were dancing on the Lord's Day, and for praying (by a form out of the end of the Common-Prayer Book) in his house and for reproving drunkards or swearers, and for talking sometimes a few words of Scripture and the life to come, he was reviled commonly by the name of Puritan, Precisian and Hypocrite: and so were the Godly Conformable Ministers that lived anywhere in the country near us.[3]

Writing after the Restoration, he described the Presbyterian system as 'but a stranger here...I found that most (that ever I could meet with) were against the *ius divinum* of lay elders and for the moderate primitive episcopacy...'.[4] Mrs Hutchinson, wife of a Baptist, also said Puritanism was commonly defined in this ethical manner:

... whoever was zealous for God's glory or worship, could not endure blasphemous oaths, ribald conversation, profane scoffs, sabbath breaking,

---

[1] I am indebted to Mr Trevor-Roper for this interpretation of the events, and also for part of the material in the preceding paragraph.

[2] *Journal of Modern History* (1942), pp. 1 ff.; *American Hist. Rev.* vol. LIII.

[3] *Reliquae Baxterianae*, I, 3.   [4] *Ibid.* p. 146.

derision of the word of God, and the like—whoever could endure a sermon, modest habit or conversation, or anything good,—all these were Puritans.[1]

The perspicacious Baillie saw in 1640 that the ways of Presbytery were not liked in England.[2] It was not on account of a desire for Presbyterianism that the attack on episcopacy was begun when the Long Parliament met. The fiercest opposition was against the political power of the bishops, rather than against their episcopal functions, and men like Bagshaw the Royalist as well as D'Ewes the Parliamentarian joined in it. D'Ewes wrote:

I desired the question to be waived in respect of the ambiguity of the matter, for if by Episcopacy is meant their vain serial titles of lordship, the spoils of the Crown with which they are loaden and their vast tyrannical power which they exercise...I gave my 'Aye' for abolishing them. But if by Episcopacy is meant only their spiritual function as it stood in primitive and purest times, then I shall give my negative voice, for I shall highly prize a godly preaching bishop, and heartily wish we might make ours such.[3]

A majority were actually opposed to episcopacy as such, however, and so the Root and Branch Petition was carried, but the surprising thing about the issue is indicated in Dering's remark on 20 November 1641:

Mr Speaker, there is a certain newborn, unseen, ignorant, dangerous, desperate way of Independency. Are we for this Independent way? Nay sir. Are we for the elder brother of it, the Presbyterial form? I have not yet heard any one gentleman within these walls stand up and assert his thoughts for either of these ways.[4]

That Dering was not simply unobservant is proved by the actual religious settlement made. The affairs of the Church were put into the hands of a commission, and it was not till the exigencies of the war forced the calling in of Scots aid that, as W. A. Shaw has shown,[5] Presbyterianism was adopted by Parliament as the price

[1] Lucy Hutchinson, *Memoirs of the Life of Colonel Hutchinson* (Everyman ed.), pp. 64–5.

[2] Baillie, *Letters and Journals*, I, 269.

[3] Quoted in W. A. Shaw, *History of the English Church during the Civil Wars*, I, 40.

[4] *Ibid.* p. 104.   [5] *Ibid.* pp. 139 ff.

for it. But it had none of the rigour of its Scottish counterpart. As Baillie said, it was 'a lame Erastian Presbytery'.[1] The Long Parliament had curbed the social and political power of the Church, which Charles had considered to be of more importance than the sword in time of peace, and it had no desire to set up a national church whose government was independent of State control and beside whose moral severity in social and political matters the Laudian consistory would seem anaemic. The majority did not want bishops; they had Presbyterianism as the cost of Scottish military aid, but they wanted to avoid the pure unadulterated Calvinist doctrine of the Church, independent of State control yet dominating the whole of life.[2]

Because in that centre of commercial capitalism, seventeenth-century England, one finds only a broken-down form of Presbyterianism, it has been said that, applied to England, Professor Tawney's thesis of the relationship between Calvinism and capitalism breaks down. But Tawney's argument is that Calvinist ethics, not Calvinist church discipline, was conducive to the spirit of capitalism. This was precisely what the Long Parliament desired. Their aim was to entrench Calvinist individualism, and at the same time to avoid Calvin's very collectivist and disciplinarian doctrine of the Church, without which Calvinism is very favourable to individualism in every sphere of life, religious and social. A running fight went on between the Long Parliament and the Westminster Assembly of Divines on this issue. When the divines won in theory it was too late to implement their system. Presbyterianism, 'that strange monster to the English people',[3] was never to be practised with any seriousness, except—how times have changed—in Lancashire and London.

THE EMERGENCE OF INDEPENDENCY

If up to the end of 1641 no one had spoken in favour of Independency in Parliament, when was this scheme of church government first seriously proposed in responsible circles? The idea was certainly widely known before, as Dering's remark indicates. Dr Ames had

---

[1] Baillie, *Letters and Journals*, II, 1.   [2] *Ibid.* p. 198.   [3] *Ibid.* p. 117.

written profusely advocating it, Laud had thought it advisable to keep a close watch on the activities of exiled Independents in Holland,[1] and of course there was the New England model, but it was not until the meeting of the Westminster Assembly that in England Independency became anything more serious than speculation.

The Westminster Assembly of Divines was in close relationship with Parliament. Appointed by Parliament it was, as Baillie lamented, 'no proper Assembly but a meeting called by the Parliament to advise them in what things they were asked'.[2] 'They have no power to write one line to any soul but as the Parliament directs.'[3] The presence of Parliamentary members made the connexion between the two bodies even closer.

The great majority of ministers at the Assembly favoured Presbyterianism. There were about a dozen Independent ministers, who adopted obstructionist tactics as the only possible method to check them. This battle at Westminster brought the issue into prominence in Parliamentary circles. Before this, episcopacy had indeed been abolished, but no policy for a positive reorganization of the Church had yet been brought forward. At the Westminster Assembly a definite proposal was made—Presbyterianism on the Scottish model —which was so distasteful to Independents and Erastians alike that they had to do something about it.

Now what was the relationship between these Independent members of the Westminster Assembly and the Independents in Parliament? The generally assumed answer was simple: that the Independent political party was, *simpliciter*, like the Independent churchmen, advocating toleration, and over this question split with the Presbyterian members of Parliament, who were not tolerant and wanted a rigid Presbyterianism. This is not a satisfactory interpretation.

In the first place, when Presbyterianism was foisted on the Long Parliament in order to secure Scottish aid, who should be the leading engineers of this covenant with Scotland but the two leading Independents, Vane and St John? Secondly, most Parliamentarians

[1] H. R. Trevor-Roper, *Archbishop Laud*, pp. 247 ff.
[2] Baillie, *Letters and Journals*, II, 186.　　[3] *Ibid*.

were demonstrably Erastian.[1] And when the Presbyterian party
had the opportunity to speak for Presbyterianism, apparently it had
remained silent. Baxter wrote of English Presbyterianism in 1660:

> Any man that was for a serious spiritual way of worship, (though he were
> for moderate episcopacy or liturgy,) and that lived according to his pro-
> fession was commonly called a Presbyterian, as formerly he was called a
> Puritan, unless he joined himself to Independents, Anabaptists or some other
> sect which might afford him a more odious name. And of the Lords, he
> that was for Episcopacy and liturgy was called a Presbyterian if he en-
> deavoured to procure any abatement of their impositions for the reconciling
> of the parties or the ease of the ministers and people that disliked them.
> And of the ministers he was called a Presbyterian that was for Episcopacy
> and liturgy if he conformed not so far as to subscribe or swear to the English
> diocesan name and all their impositions. I knew not of any one or Lord at
> court that was a Presbyterian: yet were the Earl of Manchester (a good man,)
> and the Earl of Anglesey and Lord Hollis called Presbyterians and as such
> appointed to direct and help them, when I have heard them speak for
> moderate Episcopacy and liturgy myself.[2]

When the leader of the Presbyterian party favoured episcopacy,
and in all probability assisted the Independent chaplain John Hodges
after his ejectment,[3] it is hard to describe the Presbyterian members
of Parliament as violently Presbyterian or intractably intolerant.

But it was a rather different matter with Independency. The
Independents fought tenaciously for their position, and men do not
fight so strongly for things indifferent. (Of course, the question
remains—may not this Independency for which they fought be the
rationalization for some material or political advantage?) Who in
fact were the Independents in Parliament and what did they really
want?

PROFESSOR HEXTER'S THESIS

In 1938 Professor Hexter appeared to shatter the long-accepted view
that the difference between Presbyterian and Independent parties
was on the question of toleration.[4] He had found, he stated, that
the big majority of Independent members of Parliament (and he

[1] Shaw, *op. cit.* ch. I, *passim*.   [2] *Reliquae Baxterianae*, I, 278.
[3] A. G. Matthews, *Calamy Revised*.
[4] *American Hist. Rev.* XLIV, 29 ff.

defined as Independents those who survived Pride's Purge, signed the King's death warrant or belonged to the Rump Parliament) were Presbyterian elders. Lists of the Presbyterian elders from seven counties remain, and Hexter found that of the eighty-eight members of Parliament returned by those counties, twenty-four Independents were Presbyterian elders and only six were not—as high a percentage as among Presbyterian members of Parliament. Including non-resident members, in all thirty-nine Independents were Presbyterian elders, and this out of only seven counties. Hexter explained this odd situation in the following way: Most Puritans wanted reforms in ritual and the re-affirmation of pure Calvinist doctrine. Some had, in addition, strong views on Church government, and were Erastians, Presbyterians or Independents.

While Pym dominated the House of Commons in the early years of the war, no religious divisions emerged of any consequence, and for a year after his death a man's religious ardour rather than his ecclesiastical theories still determined his party allegiance. All the militant Puritans were united in the godly party as opposed to the moderates. They attempted to discredit the Earl of Essex and succeeded in doing so when he was defeated at Lostwithiel. 'Immediately thereafter, toward the end of 1644 the "godly party" was torn asunder...by the emergence of the religious issue in an acute form.' (But Hexter does not really say what caused this issue to emerge.)

The Erastians and most Puritans joined with the real Presbyterians to set up Presbyterianism, and then, changing tactics, joined with the Independents to take the sting out of it, to make it a 'lame Erastian Presbytery'. Consequently, the seventy-five per cent of Independents on Hexter's list became elders without violating party policy.

The leaders of the Independents, Vane and St John, seeing the imminent breakdown of the godly party in 1644, engineered the Self-Denying Ordinance to check the swing of the balance of power to the Presbyterians. By this the Army came under the control of Independents, but as the Army was too Independent, it alienated the majority of Puritans in the House. The real Independents, unable to get a majority in either House, had to stand by the Army. The split in the godly party forced Vane and St John to abandon the Scots, who allied with the moderates and Presbyterians, but this alliance was overawed by force in 1647 and finally broken by Pride's Purge. There was never a clear-cut religious issue between real Presbyterianism and real Independency. The average Puritan member of Parliament, Hexter continued, 'had to choose rather between the flaccid trussed-up Presbyterianism...and the continually fluctuating program of the Independents'. The Commonwealth was supported for a variety of reasons—'Independency', Republicanism or self-interest—but the name Independent was a mere label, applied without discrimination by one's enemies.

At first sight Hexter's thesis, based on the evidence he puts forward, appears incontrovertible, but further evidence leads to a different conclusion. It is true that many Independents became temporarily Presbyterian elders, but by and large they belonged to the conservative wing of the party. Before 1650 there was no real alternative open to most but to choose either Presbyterianism or Brownism. The conservative Independents chose the former, the radical the latter; but after 1650 they could, and in fact did, choose the 'very middle way' of Independency. Let us turn to Hexter's thesis in detail. First, there are a few errors of identification.

Of the thirty-nine Independents whom he lists as elders in presbyteries,[1] William Ball had died in 1648;[2] it is doubtful whether Edmund Harvey the Suffolk elder is the same Edmund Harvey, member of Parliament for Great Bedwin, silk-merchant and partner of Alderman Sleigh of London; Sir Roger North, probably excluded at Pride's Purge, did not return to the House afterwards;[3] John Harrington, member of Parliament for Somerset, was a most Presbyterian Presbyterian, certainly absent during Pride's Purge and apparently not returning; and Henry Weston the recruiter member of Parliament for Guildford was excluded at Pride's Purge and does not appear on any committee of the Rump, although he was

[1] For evidence on the names in this section see Appendix A, except where otherwise stated.

[2] *Commons Journals*, 8 May 1648.

[3] I am indebted to Mr D. H. Pennington of the University of Manchester for the information about North, Harrington and Weston. Sir Roger North is on one list only of re-admitted members, but does not appear on any committee of the Rump.

certainly friendly with Cromwell, and indeed installed, at his request, a parish minister who was unlikely to be a Presbyterian.[1]

Secondly, the remainder, almost to a man, were the less radical Independents. Six were probably excluded by Pride's Purge— John Ashe, Nathaniel Bacon, Sir William Brereton, Peter Brooke, William Ellis and Brampton Gurdon. Of the rest, thirteen were absent at Pride's Purge and had no connexion with the King's trial—Robert Brewster, Thomas Fell, John and Robert Goodwin, Lislebone Long, Sir William Masham and his son, John Palmer, Alexander and Edward Popham, John Pyne and Benjamin Weston. Sir John Barrington retired from politics immediately after the purge. Six refused to be King's judges—John Corbet, John Gurdon, Roger Hill, Edmund Prideaux, Alexander Rigby and Robert Reynolds. Four more surviving the Purge had nothing to do with the Trial—Robert Blake, George Serle, George Snelling and George Thompson. Four were King's Judges but refused to sign the Death Warrant—Francis Allen, William Heveningham, Sir Henry Mildmay and Sir Thomas Wrothe. John Moore was the name of the only Presbyterian elder on Hexter's list who survived Pride's Purge and signed the Death Warrant as well—that is, if this head of a family of 'arrant thieves... profane bitter scoffers at piety'[2] was indeed the elder of the Fifth Lancashire classis. One would not be surprised if such a one changed sides with circumstances. In any case, there was not an Independent congregation near Liverpool to which he could have belonged whatever his inclinations.

As only five, that is, fourteen per cent, of those in Hexter's list had anything to do with the King's trial, compared with the figure of nearer forty per cent of the Independent party as a whole, it is clear that the vast majority of this sample of 'Presbyterian Independents' were not radical. As far as I can judge, the really radical Independents in religion and politics, by and large, never countenanced Presbyterianism.

It is significant that although many Independents were Presbyterian elders, I have found no instance of a supporter of political Presbyterianism who was either an Independent or Separatist in

[1] *Writings and Speeches of Oliver Cromwell*, ed. Abbott, III, 120.
[2] *The Moore Rental* (Chetham Soc. vol. XII).

religion. Further, of the extremely radical Independents, those who signed the King's death warrant, only two out of fifty-nine (Moore and Anthony Stapley) were religious Presbyterians—and doubtful cases at that—whereas I have found nearly thirty who were religious Independents or Separatists.

In a sense the significant Independents were the early ones—those members of Parliament who fled to the Army in 1647 when the Presbyterians in Parliament seemed all-powerful—because they threw their lot in with the party before it was evident that it would be successful. In this group, the overwhelming majority of those whose religious affiliation I have been able to trace were Independents or sectaries.[1]

Further investigation of the religious affiliations of those on Hexter's list reveals that nearly half, at least, either became Independents or Separatists or had some connexion with them. This might be thought to support Hexter's hypothesis, but another explanation than that given by him is more likely. Of those whom I have been able to trace—Allen, Bacon, Harvey (if he is the Suffolk elder), Rigby and Reynolds probably became Independents; Sir William Brereton had an Independent chaplain; Roger Williams himself was chaplain to the Masham family for some years, and John Owen, the leading Independent minister, dedicated his book *Ebenezer* to Sir William Masham in 1648; George Thomson became a Fifth Monarchy man; Thomas Fell's wife was a Quaker and Quaker meetings were held in his house, although he never became one himself; Brampton Gurdon had been tutored in 1634 by Henry Jessey who was soon to become a very radical Baptist, while both Brampton and his brother John were close friends of the Independent, Governor Winthrop of Massachusetts; Edmund Prideaux's son was an Independent minister; Sir John Barrington made an Independent, John Warren, lecturer in his locality in 1643, and when the vicar departed, installed him in the living; at Wrentham, the Brewster family had John Philip, an early Independent, installed in the local church. With no evidence found to the contrary, it is very likely that William Heveningham, the lord of the manor, was involved

[1] Four Presbyterians and thirty-three certain or probable Independents. See Appendix A, p. 129, for the evidence.

when a Congregational church was set up at Heveningham soon after the local Presbyterian minister departed for Cornwall in 1650 at the instigation of one of the leading 'eleven' Presbyterian members of Parliament, Anthony Nicol. There were other similar occurrences. A Presbyterian, Humphrey Maddison, was minister at Wanstead, Essex,[1] the home of Sir Henry Mildmay, who could hardly eject the man, but who replaced him on his death or departure in 1648, by, first, Paul Amyraut,[2] one of the refugees from Laud in Holland, and in 1656 by an Independent, Leonard Hoar.[3] If he was not inclined to Independency it would be difficult to explain why Mildmay had sent his son to Harvard in 1644 to receive the pure doctrine of New England.

The situation at Wrentham is particularly interesting. In 1609 the Brewsters had installed John Philip, a radical Puritan, but their influence could not save him from Laud and in 1638, after corresponding with the prominent Independent Peters about joining him in the Netherlands, he finally went to Massachusetts. He became minister at Salem, returning to the parish church at Wrentham in 1642. He was consulted by the gathered Congregational church at Norwich, which freely permitted their members to join the Wrentham parish church, a sign of approval of his Independency.[4] Baillie recognized him as one of the Independents at the Westminster Assembly.[5] Yet both John Philip himself, as well as Robert Brewster, were members of the fifth division of the Suffolk Presbyterian classis![6] As the majority of Puritans had remained within the Laudian church because it was the church established, so, presumably, men who favoured Independency might stay within the Presbyterian church because it was the established one. For people to whom a close connexion between Church and State was of the very fabric of society, the maintenance of the parochial system would be more important than any change in ecclesiastical organization they might desire—which, indeed, would be at the same time a change in social organization. Consequently, Brewster

[1] Shaw, *op. cit.* II, 375.   [2] *Calamy Revised.*   [3] *Ibid.*
[4] J. Browne, *Congregational Churches of Norfolk and Suffolk*, pp. 421 ff.
[5] Baillie, *Letters and Journals*, II, 110.
[6] Shaw, *op. cit.* II, 425.

and Philip, though Independent, remained within the established church system. Sir John Barrington also installed an Independent (John Warren) as parish minister,[1] and both men were members of the Essex presbytery.[2]

Other Independent ministers who were also members of presbyteries included Joseph Caryl,[3] Seth Wood[4] and William Strong, minister of St Dunstan's-in-the-West,[5] where Francis Allen, the Independent member of Parliament, was an elder.

By 1650, lacking government support, Presbyterianism began to decay and was obviously not the national church in any real sense. Those Independents who had formerly supported it in order to avoid Separatism could now be Independents openly, for Independency had become the 'established' religion, if anything was. This surely explains the huge increase in the number of Independent congregations after 1650. It was not due to mass conversion. The greater part of the increase came about through parish churches changing from Presbyterian to Independent, because the incipient Independency growing within the parish churches in the previous decade could now implement itself, while still preserving the parish church model.

The truth is that the Presbyterian Independents referred to by Hexter represented the politically and religiously conservative wing of the party. There was a more radical wing, but in order to understand the part played by it, we must trace the history of Independency.

HOW AND WHEN DID INDEPENDENCY BECOME AN ISSUE IN PARLIAMENT?

Independency was known in England before 1640 and particularly influenced some members of the Providence Company who played a conspicuous part in the Civil War, for example, Lord Brooke. Nye and Goodwin[6] had a great influence when they returned from

[1] S. Palmer, *Nonconformist Memorials*, II, 201.
[2] Shaw, *op. cit.* II, 382.   [3] *Ibid.* p. 401.
[4] *Ibid.* p. 429.   [5] *Ibid.* p. 404.
[6] Incidentally, Nye was nominated for the Westminster Assembly by the members of Parliament of Huntingdonshire (two of whom were Valentine Walton and Abraham Burrell), and Thomas Goodwin by those of Cambridgeshire, Cromwell's county. *Commons Journals*, 20 April 1642, 23 April 1642.

exile in 1640 and their enemies charged them with deliberate proselytizing among influential people.

Most parliament supporters in the Commons were Puritan and anti-episcopalian, but not committed to any other form of church organization, as Dering's remark indicates. Vane was almost the only member of the Commons who had any knowledge from experience on the subject, through his life in the colonies.[1] The matter was not brought into prominence by the death of Pym, as Hexter seems to suggest,[2] but by the Scots Covenant and the calling of the Westminster Assembly. Baillie wrote in December 1643: 'The Independents, being most able men and of great credit, fearing no less than banishment from their native country if Presbyteries were erected, are watchful that no conclusion be taken for their prejudice.'[3] It was largely a matter of fear. The Laudian persecution, that had fallen most heavily on Separatists and Independents, was very recent. When under the Laudian regime, men like Lord Say and Sele, Lord Brooke, Darley, Cromwell and Vane either migrated or thought of migrating for largely religious reasons,[4] it is hardly likely that they would face the prospect of another religious auto-cracy with equanimity.

Their position was difficult. The war must be won, to prevent any return to Charles' paternal government. There must be no dangerous compromise peace. In the early days the Independents tended to be of the war party or on the left of the middle group. The Scottish alliance was necessary to win the war, but was fraught with danger, because Presbyterianism might not grant sufficient flexibility in religious matters.

The commission to Scotland to arrange the Covenant consisted of Vane, Darley, Armine and Nye, all Independents, Marshall (Nye's father-in-law), and Hatcher, a half-hearted Presbyterian.[5] It is unlikely that this choice was fortuitous. The persons mentioned

[1] *D.N.B.*

[2] *Op. cit.* p. 42. I may have misunderstood Hexter on this point, but I cannot see from his argument why hostility between the two groups should have broken out at this juncture.

[3] Baillie, *Letters and Journals*, II, 116.

[4] A. P. Newton, *Colonising Activities of the English Puritans*, p. 245.

[5] Baillie, *Letters and Journals*, II, 89.

were not simply from the war party. The significant fact is that at this stage Vane, Darley and Armine were on the left of the middle group. Vane adroitly changed the wording of the Covenant so that reformation in the Church was not to be Presbyterianism *simpliciter*, but 'according to the Word of God',[1] which afforded a good debating ground for the Independent ministers at Westminster. It is possible that this episode should be regarded as marking the birth of the Independent political party. In any case, within a few months, the Independents of the Westminster Assembly were linked with a political group in Parliament. A pamphlet dated November 1643 spoke of the fear that the Independents might attempt to hinder the Scottish alliance.[2] By October 1643 it had become common knowledge that they formed a distinct group. This was the time when Ogle formed his plan to unite Royalists and Independents against the Presbyterians. He wrote to Lord Bristol:

> The party here that have incensed and maintained this war consists of three sorts of people. The first and greatest are the moderate zealous protestants, lovers (though desirous of some amendment) of the Common Prayer Book. The second and next considerable to this are the rigid Presbyterians. The third are the Independents and Brownists, among whom do some few and very inconsiderable anabaptists and other fantastic sectaries mix themselves.[3]

While Ogle was sounding Nye and Goodwin to discover whether they would make a truce with the King, overtures were made through Lord Lovelace to the younger Vane. The latter was known 'to have a strong party in the House and to be the chief of it'.[4] And it was of Vane that 'Anti-Aulicus' wrote that the King, 'having taken notice of him and others of his judgment and conceiving them to be real and hearts in their intention, did promise them liberty of conscience'.[5] There was known, that is to say, to be a connexion between the Independent ministers and a group in the House which must already have had some cohesion.

D'Ewes also used the term Independents of the 'violent spirits' by

---

[1] S. R. Gardiner, *History of the Great Civil War*, II, 230, 234.
[2] Thomason, *Tracts*, E 75 (22).
[3] *Camden Society Miscellany* (1883), p. 3.
[4] *Ibid.* p. xi.   [5] *Ibid.* p. xiii.

24 August 1643.[1] When the peace party peers, Bedford and Holland, went to Oxford in August 1643, Northumberland more cautiously went to his county seat at Petworth to see how they fared, and who should accompany him but Sir John Evelyn of Wiltshire, later to be regarded as a leading radical? Evelyn wrote to his uncle Sir John of Surrey, urging him in guarded terms to make his peace with the King, as he himself intended to do. The letter was intercepted by Parliamentary soldiers under the radical Colonel Herbert Morley, who were presumably in the neighbourhood in order to make Northumberland hesitate over any rash decision. Evelyn promptly returned to Westminster, and to get out of trouble, joined the war party, and most significantly D'Ewes adds, he 'became an opponent of the Presbyterian Church government'.[2]

These facts show a close connexion between the war party and Independency. In the city, also, radicalism in politics accompanied religious radicalism. Describing the role of London as the centre of the Grand Rebellion, 'Mercurius Civicus' said that the military preparation of the city 'had affected little, had not fire been given from the pulpit',[3] and that the ringleaders particularly sought for positions of authority those who 'had seen Amsterdam or had been an Adventurer to New England or had been the post of the silenced ministers'.[4] And whom should he name as one of the chief preachers of disloyalty but Mr Hugh Peters?[5] This was no idle Royalist gossip. A group of citizens of 'good quality', the 'most active and most religious part of the city', under the leadership of Mr Shute, presented frequent petitions to the House of Commons from November 1642 onwards, urging it to beware of 'accommodation', to see that the malignant party shared in the cost of the war, and that Puritan ideals were enforced.[6] They denied, on 21 November 1642,

[1] D'Ewes Journal, Harleian MSS. 165, folio 156. (I am indebted to Dr C. M. Williams for this and the following reference.)

[2] *Ibid.* folios 157 ff. This section was possibly inserted nine months after the date, and it is impossible to say with certainty if he used the term Independent in 1643 or whether it was not commonly used until 1644 and he was writing it back into the events. See also Gardiner, *op. cit.* I, 199.

[3] 'Mercurius Civicus to Mercurius Rusticus', Somers, *Tracts*, IV, 585.

[4] *Ibid.* p. 582.   [5] *Ibid.* p. 588.

[6] *Commons Journals*, 13 Nov. 1642.

that they were Independents,[1] a denial understandable at a stage when Independency was equated with Brownism, but one that can carry little weight, for when again in March 1643 Mr Shute and others brought a very radical petition before the London Council, alleging among other things that the present evils of the kingdom were due not to evil counsellors but to the King himself, who should be at the council door urging the aldermen to support the petition but 'that Peters, one of the Amsterdamians that now rules the roost'?[2] So, again, there is a connexion between an Independent minister and radical opinion.

Certainly the great majority of the war party in the Commons were leading political Independents of the later years of the Long Parliament. Marten, Mildmay, Wentworth, Haselrig, Holland, Morley, Rigby, Prideaux, Gurdon, Miles Corbet, Denis Bond, Hoyle, Blackston, Masham, Heyman and Pennington[3] were all important Independents from 1645-8. All but Marten, Wentworth, Baynton, Hoyle and Heyman[4] were certainly convinced Puritans, and Marten, who was 'so far from a Puritan as light from darkness', yet certainly favoured toleration. Of the strong Puritans among them, only Corbet and Pennington were indisputably Independent, though there is evidence that the others would favour that view. But as Dering noted, in the early years of the Long Parliament, they were not advocating classical Independency. They wanted a measure of toleration, although I doubt whether they would have gone as far as the Independents in the Army who held that no man should be bound or tied to anything, but every man left free to hold what he pleased.

Independency was more adaptable to toleration than Presbyterianism. In the early stages of the Westminster Assembly, the Independent ministers were at pains to dissociate themselves from the radical sects,[5] but as they became aware of the hopelessness of their outnumbered position, they sought allies wherever they could find them, in Parliament, in the Army and among the sectaries. To

---

[1] *Ibid.* 14 Dec. 1642.   [2] 'Mercurius Aulicus', 2 April 1643, p. 170.
[3] The names of the war party are taken from Hexter, *The Reign of King Pym*.
[4] I have no evidence one way or the other as to these five.
[5] Baillie, *Letters and Journals*, II, 121.

do this, they were forced to move much closer to a policy of general toleration, which indeed appeared to be all they could hope for. As far as one can judge from Baillie's letters, their policy was to have toleration granted by Parliament before Presbyterianism was set up.[1] And, as a tiny minority in the early days of the Long Parliament, this was essentially all they strove for.

Thus the Independent ministers at the Westminster Assembly aimed for some sort of toleration, and, remembering their exile, tended to be radical. The Independents in Parliament, although at first they were not to be identified with the war party, saw that Scots help was necessary to prevent defeat, and so entered into the covenant with Presbyterians. But in order to combat the rigorous intolerance of Presbyterianism, they backed the Independents of the Assembly, and to gain sufficient strength, had to ally themselves with the radicals of the Army and of Parliament.

[1] Baillie, *Letters and Journals*, II, 230.

CHAPTER IV

The Composition and Aims of the Party

SOCIAL COMPOSITION

THE question still remains, who were these Independents? Mr Trevor-Roper, who accepted the evidence of Hexter's article, and therefore abandoned the old, purely religious, division between Independents and Presbyterians, in his important article on the Gentry[1] defined the Independents as a social group consisting of the lesser gentry. In this article, he held that the gentry in the late sixteenth and early seventeenth centuries were on the whole declining, and only those able to secure some remunerative office, the 'court gentry', were the rising gentry. (His wide definition of 'court gentry' includes all holding lucrative official posts either in London or the provinces, indeed, almost all with income from sources other than land or trade, 'local office as well as central office, country lawyers as well as London city lawyers, deputy sheriffs as well as ministers'.[2]) The rest were declining gentry, mere gentry, lesser gentry, country gentry, who, with rising prices, without remunerative office, could not continue living on their former lavish scale, but, especially from the time of James I, found it increasingly difficult to break into the favoured circles. They were without the former opportunities provided to take up church livings, under-rented lands, stewardships and titles since the work of Bancroft to conserve church property; they were debarred from privateering since the peace with Spain; and they were finding the exactions, such as wardship, heavier. The country gentry could not make ends meet, and consequently they became more radical in politics. Hence the Essex revolt, and the spasmodic risings of Midland gentry after James' accession. Hence also the rise of the Independent men who more than any others made the Great

---

[1] 'The Gentry 1540–1640', *Economic History Review* Supplement (1953).
[2] *Ibid.* p. 27.

Rebellion, men whose radicalism converted it from a series of political manœuvres into a Civil War.[1]

There is obviously evidence to support this suggestive hypothesis. Many Independents were, as was to be expected in that pyramid-like society, lesser gentry, but there were lesser gentry in the ranks of the Presbyterians and Royalists too. The question would arise as to whether the lesser gentry were represented in the Independent party to a larger extent than in any other, and, if they were, was this greater representation significant enough to enable them to voice their aims and aspirations?

Who, precisely, are the 'lesser gentry'? Can one safely use the terms 'lesser gentry', 'mere gentry', 'declining gentry', as synonymous for country gentlemen? A declining peer is still not the same social genus as a lesser gentleman whose fortunes may not be falling. Nor are social and economic categories interchangeable. As Thomas Wilson pointed out in 1600,[2] a gentleman who was accounted rich in the North of England would be of no economic account in the South, although his social standing in the North might be very great. Was he a greater or a lesser gentleman?

Apart from these difficulties of definition, other points must be considered. First, Mr Trevor-Roper does not explain why the declining recusant gentry were such ardent Royalists; surely the abolition of the Court of Wards would have been worth a sermon. Finally, it leaves unanswered the question why so many of the early Independents were not lesser gentlemen; why some declining gentry left the party just as it came to power; and why the actual regicides were political and religious radicals almost to a man, while those Independent gentry who were less radical in religion drew back at this point.

It is important to distinguish between the early Independents and members of the party who subsequently supported the Rump. Until 1647 the future success of the Independents was far from obvious. In the list of those who fled to the Army in 1647 there are the names of many lesser gentry, but it also includes a high per-

---

[1] 'The Gentry 1540–1640', *Economic History Review* Supplement (1953), p. 33.
[2] 'The State of England', *Camden Society Miscellany* (1936), p. 24.

centage of the upper gentry.[1] Cases in point are Sir William Armine of Osgodby, Lincolnshire, Sheriff of the county; John Bamfield, heir to rich estates at Poltimore, Devon; John Bingham of Bingham Melcombe, of an ancient Dorset family; Henry Darley, New England adventurer and heir to Buttercrombe, Yorkshire; Edmund Dunch, Sheriff of Berkshire, son and heir of Sir William Dunch of Little Wittenham; Nathaniel and John Fiennes, sons of Lord Say and Sele; Lord Grey of Groby; Sir Arthur Haselrig, owner of great estates; Lord Lisle; Simon Mayne, lord of Dinton Manor near Aylesbury; Oliver St John, son of Lord St John; Augustine Skinner of Totesham Hall, East Farleigh, Kent, who paid £5665 for the lands of the Bishop of Rochester; Francis Thornaugh, one of the greater gentry of Nottingham; and John Trenchard, heir to the estates of an ancient Dorset family.

All the above were either certainly or probably in sympathy with religious Independency. To these may be added the following about whose religious affiliations I have little evidence. John Evelyn of Wiltshire; Roger Hill,[2] landed lawyer of Poundisford, Devon, who later acquired Taunton Dene, one of the richest manors in the country; Sir Thomas Jervois, a rich landowner of Hampshire, and a relative of the Marquis of Winchester; William Lemon, nephew of the Puritan Mayor of London, Sir John Lemon, whose estates he inherited, in addition to Eastchurch manors in Kent; Henry Marten, whose income was at least £3000 per annum; Lord Monson; Sir Gregory Norton, with estates in Berkshire, Buckingham and Kent; William Pierpoint, son of the Earl of Kingston, who married into the Tonge estates in Shropshire; Robert Wallop, son of one of the wealthiest commoners in England; and Benjamin Weston, fourth son of the Duke of Portland. Such persons cannot plausibly be considered as 'declining gentry'. One cannot dogmatize until much more is known of their fortunes—a fair test would perhaps be an income of £2000 per annum, but they would certainly appear

[1] Documentation of the following lists is given in Appendix A and p. 129, setting out the whole party in a series of tables.

[2] Clement Walker (*History of Independency*, I, 167), claims that Hill had but a mean estate before the war. This may be true but he certainly was from an ancient county family. See Brunton and Pennington, *Members of the Long Parliament*, p. 165.

to be quite as socially important as most Presbyterians. As they comprise nearly half of the early Parliamentary Independent supporters, in what sense can they be said to represent an opposite social group to the Presbyterians? Did they in any real sense represent or share in the social aspirations of some of the 'declining' and lesser gentry of the party? I have no evidence to suggest that they did.

Some of these early Independents were in financial difficulties and could well be labelled 'declining'. For instance, Sir William Constable, Sir John Danvers and Sir Peter Temple were all deeply in debt. It is also true that others may fairly be regarded as 'lesser gentry'. Examples are Miles Corbet, Recorder of Yarmouth; Cornelius Holland, 'the creature of Vane'; Gervase Piggotts of Nottinghamshire; Thomas Lister, Edmund Ludlow, Thomas Scott, Henry Smith, whose Leicester manor was worth £600 per annum, all of whom were probably Independent in religion; John Corbet and Humphrey Edwards of Shropshire; Philip Smith of unknown origin; John Weaver of Lincolnshire; Thomas Wogan of Pembroke and Lawrence Whitacre. The merchant members, again, included lesser merchants, probably Independent in religion, such as Francis Allen, alderman of London; Blackston, mercer of Newcastle; and Thomas Boone, merchant of Devon. Some Independents, to turn to another group represented by Oliver St John, Roger Hill, Bulstrode Whitelocke and Edmund Prideaux, were lawyers, but it is a question whether it would be correct to call them 'lesser lawyers'. What criterion of 'greater' or 'lesser' should be applied?

In addition to those who fled to the Army in 1647, other early Independents were Sir Henry Vane, junior, one of the leading gentlemen of the kingdom; William Heveningham, a very substantial landowner of Suffolk; and Isaac Pennington, the wealthy former Mayor of London. Vane and Pennington were certainly religiously radical, while I think it likely that Heveningham at least favoured Independency.

Possibly eighty per cent, and certainly seventy per cent, of these were sympathetic to Independency. A very substantial percentage were as much 'greater gentry' as were the Presbyterians, and I should be inclined to say that the reasons for their party affiliation were ideological—an attachment to Independency or Republicanism or

oppty for lesser.

both. But it is significant that many of the greater gentry of the party dropped out when events took a very radical turn. Sir William Armine, Bamfield, Sir John Evelyn, Nathaniel and John Fiennes, and Augustine Skinner took little part in the Rump, while Bingham, Boone, Darley, Haselrig, Jervois, Lemon, Pierpoint, St John, Vane and Weston were absent from Pride's Purge and the King's trial. By that time the leadership had passed from Vane and St John to Cromwell and Ireton.

Some of the 'declining gentry' backed out of affairs just at the very moment of the party's triumph, when they might reasonably have expected the fruits of victory, with lucrative offices and monetary rewards which would have arrested their decline. Sir Peter Temple of Stowe, Buckinghamshire, one of the leading gentry of the county, of a family raised to eminence in the sixteenth century, and sheriff in 1635, was indebted to the extent of £20,000 despite an income of £3500. He fled to the Army in 1647[1] and was considered sufficiently radical to be nominated a King's judge. Yet after Pride's Purge he dropped out of affairs completely. Sir John Barrington, one of the leading gentry of Essex, with estates in Hertfordshire as well, withdrew almost entirely after the King's death, although he was in debt for £10,000. His family remained financially embarrassed for the next decade. They were strong Puritans. His father had been engaged with Pym in colonizing activity, and he himself was an Independent and a cousin of Cromwell. It was surely these convictions and connexions, and not the fact that he was a 'declining gentleman' which led to his early allegiance to the Independent party. The same economic considerations are also true of William, Lord Monson. He had at one time vied with Buckingham for the position of court favourite; had married into large estates in Surrey, and was extremely radical up to the time of Pride's Purge. Yet he tended to drop out of affairs after the King's trial, although he was in financial difficulties, and in 1659 was imprisoned for debt. Algernon Sidney, second son of the Earl of Leicester, took a somewhat similar course. Though he bemoaned his lack of estates, he refused, nevertheless, to have anything to do with Charles' death and played little part in the Republic.

[1] This may be his namesake, the member of Parliament for Leicester.

On the other hand, Sir John Danvers, who 'by a vain expense in his way of living had contracted a vast debt', and Sir William Constable, member of an ancient but decayed family, went to the extreme length of signing Charles' death warrant. No doubt, there were other members of the party in a similar economic predicament. But if the rise of the party is to be explained by the fact that it was the party of the declining and lesser gentry, then how can one possibly account for the early adherence of those who backed out of affairs at the very moment when it looked as if their financial problems would be solved?

A third point is somewhat puzzling. If the Independents were a country party, jibbing at the tenacious and increasing sway of London, where Presbyterianism 'had a notorious power', why is it that such leading London citizens as Isaac Pennington, Samuel Moyer, Rowland Wilson, John Foulkes, and William Gibbs supported the party even before Pride's Purge? Clearly in view of their record they cannot be said to be pure financial opportunists, like some other London merchants such as Sir Thomas Viner, Abraham Burrell, Christopher Packe and Robert Andrews, who sided with whoever was in power with apparent ease. Moyer, Pennington and Wilson were religious radicals, while Pennington, Gibbs and Foulkes had committed themselves to the radical cause so early that there was no turning back for them. Why had they done this?

Besides these great merchants there were many other London citizens of some distinction: Alderman Francis Allen, an instrument of the Independents even before he was a member of Parliament; Alderman Atkins, Mayor 1644–5; Praise-God Barbon, the substantial leather-seller of Fleet Street; John Barkstead, the goldsmith; Owen Rowe, the silk-mercer; John Venn, warden of the Merchant Taylors Company—all radicals in religion as well as early radicals in politics—while Edmund Harvey and Nicholas Gold were also early supporters of the Independents.

One might expect the merchants of the country towns to be Independents, being jealous of Presbyterian London. Many were, but Matthew Allen, brewer and alderman of Weymouth; Samuel Clerke, merchant of Exeter; Robert Ellison of Newcastle; Thomas Gell, Recorder of Derby, and second son of Sir Thomas; Giles

Green, Town Clerk of Weymouth; William Jesson, Mayor of Coventry; John Nixon, alderman of Oxford; John Nash, a Worcester clothier; George Scutt, merchant of Poole; and Simon Snow, Mayor of Exeter, were all excluded at Pride's Purge; and so, presumably, were political Presbyterians.[1]

There were proportionately about the same number of provincial merchants in each party, but whereas those adhering to the Presbyterians were largely obscure, I think it is true to say that many of the Independent merchants took a more active part in proceedings, for example, Sir William Allanson, Mayor of York; John Blackston, merchant of Newcastle; Robert Blake the Admiral, formerly a merchant of Bridgwater; Thomas Boone, a Devon merchant; Denis Bond, a clothier of Dorchester and member of the Dorchester colonizing company; Daniel Blagrave, Recorder of Reading; Nathaniel Hallowes, Mayor of Derby 1657; Thomas Harrison, son of a rich butcher of Newcastle under Lyme; Thomas Purey, alderman of Gloucester; Francis Thorpe, Recorder of Beverley (who were all Independents and religious radicals), and Richard Aldworth, Bristol merchant; the Ashe family of Somerset, London and Kent; John Dove the careerist alderman of Salisbury; Alderman Hoyle of York, who, instead of cashing in on the Republic, 'hanged himself in remorse on the anniversary of the King's death';[2] John Palmer the apothecary of Taunton; John Radcliffe, alderman of Chester; George Serle, Mayor of Taunton; Thomas Toll, alderman of King's Lynn; and the Recorder of Richmond, John Wastell. (If the Presbyterians had remained in power, of course, the situation might have been reversed, and these might have been the obscure people.)

I can find little sociological difference between this group and the Presbyterians from the provincial towns. The solution may, of course, be simple. Just as Blackston was in the orbit of Haselrig's influence, others may have been dominated by some leading Presbyterian. We do not yet know enough about these men to be able to work out the systems of patronage in the Long Parliament.

[1] The information about these members is from the W. D. Pink MSS., John Rylands Library, Manchester, and from Miss C. V. Wedgwood's notes at the Institute of Historical Research.

[2] J. Vicars, *Dagon Demolished* (1660).

AIMS OF THE GROUPS

The Independents' programme was not sufficiently uniform, except in the question of religious toleration, to bear out, without important modification, Mr Trevor-Roper's hypothesis that it was the party of decentralization. He sums up their programme: 'Where were the Independents heading? They did not know...but they knew what they hated'—the Court with its office holders, lawyers, pensioners and privileged monopolists; the peers; the City; the feudal dues of wardship and purveyance; and the Church of Bancroft and Laud. In their place they preached decentralization: decentralization of government, religion, trade, law and education, while finally their foreign policy was to be a return to the Elizabethan privateering war with Spain.[1]

But, with the exception of religion, these demands were either rejected by important groups of Independents, or else were also accepted by non-Independents. They are either too exclusive or too inclusive to summarize the aims of the Independents, although any one of them would have had much support from many of that party. Did they all, for example, want decentralization of trade?

'I thought', protested a gentleman of Dorset, 'that long ere this we should have the trade dispersed all the nation over; and this City, it seems, must have all the trade.'[2] True enough, this gentleman from Dorset, Denis Bond, was a leading and consistent Independent. Yet whom should he be opposing but Aldermen Foote, Foulkes, and Packe, three leading City Independents, the first two of whom, indeed, were early and radical members of the party.[3] The politics of the City are an issue about which we know so little that the point should not be pressed too strongly, but if decentralization had been a chief aim of the Independents, the presence of such a strong group of them in London, men such as Pennington, Rowland Wilson, Robert Andrews and Slingsby Bethel, needs explanation. Under Cromwell, indeed, there is much evidence to support the view that the Independents did want decentralization, and that the regime was

[1] Trevor-Roper, *Archbishop Laud*, pp. 42–3.
[2] Burton, *Parliamentary Diary*, I, 177.
[3] Walker, *op. cit.* II, 185.

not really supported by the City merchants.[1] Yet that pure Independent Republic, the Rump government, adopted a policy of economic imperialism which certainly had much greater support in the City than did any policy of Cromwell, and it was the City alone that petitioned in favour of the Rump at their expulsion.

The last fact is important. Were the Independents the party of decentralization, as has been claimed, and the Presbyterians the party of London and centralization? Undoubtedly many Independents did want decentralization, but would not this desire be shared by the country supporters of the Presbyterians, the many provincial merchants excluded at Pride's Purge?[2] In his 'Good Work for a Good Magistrate',[3] Hugh Peters, one of the leading Independent theorists and himself a west countryman, certainly urged reform of the law; the mitigation of the ruinous legal fees; the decentralization of the universities; but he also urged the building of 'a large brave quay' on the Thames to improve the port of London.

Cromwell certainly trebled the county seats and slashed the borough seats, but if this was simply in the interests of decentralization, why did Richard Cromwell reverse the policy?[4]

The Independents were not alone in wishing to decentralize education—so too did Richard Baxter, who was not of that party; and on the question of the peerage they were obviously divided. Independent peers like Lords Say and Sele and Wharton did not want their own abolition;[5] Cromwell and Ireton at the Putney Debates seemed to oppose the Levellers on the subject of the Lords' veto;[6] and Cromwell in power sought to restore the peerage, which, to the Republican Independents, was a return to bondage and Egypt.[7]

---

[1] M. P. Ashley, *Financial and Commercial Policy under the Cromwellian Protectorate*, p. 16.

[2] See above, pp. 52–3.

[3] Written in 1651 for 'regulating most cares of the Commonwealth', B.M. 516. a. 45.

[4] J. R. Tanner, *Constitutional Conflicts of the Seventeenth Century*, p. 203.

[5] C. H. Firth, *The House of Lords during the Civil War*, pp. 250–1.

[6] Woodhouse, *Puritanism and Liberty*, p. 88.

[7] Burton, *op. cit.* II, 403.

If the Independents, again, were enthusiastic about reform and decentralization of the law, those in power in the Rump did not show it, and turned down even Cromwell's hardly radical proposals for law reform. And, if their party platform was against monopolies, why did the monopolists old Sir Henry Vane, Sir Henry Mildmay, Sir John Hippsley, Cornelius Holland and Lawrence Whitacre support it?[1]

In one important respect or another, the programme outlined in Mr Trevor-Roper's thesis runs counter to the interests of every big group among the Independents. The London Independents, the conservative constitutionalists like Lord Say and Sele, or the Cromwellians striving for order and good government, or even the Rumper body, would each repudiate some big section of such a programme.

Exceptions do not of course invalidate the thesis, provided there was a solid core in the party giving substantial support to the programme. Big sections obviously did support substantial parts of it, and it is significant that it seems to fit most closely to the ideals of the two most classical Independents, Ireton and Peters, though I know of no evidence to suggest that they wanted decentralization of trade. But the evidence as to the aims of a solid core is still too scanty and uncertain for a final statement to be made.

These criticisms, however, can be partially met by emphasizing the composite character of the Independent party. It was a composite group in two rather different ways. In the first place, it combined men of both radical and conservative outlooks, politically and socially, because they were sufficiently radical in religion to object to the centralized Calvinism of Presbyterianism, although even in that sphere some were much more radical than others. Nevertheless, by comparison with the Presbyterians, they were all religious radicals.

It was a composite party, in the second place, in the sense that its members were associated in it for different reasons. It included men like Cromwell, feeling strongly about certain Independent tenets;

[1] Monopolists according to 'The Legall Fundamentall Liberties of the People of England', *The Leveller Tracts 1647–1653*, ed. Haller, p. 431. See also Walker, *op. cit.* II, 147.

like Ireton, who believed Independency and a State Church to be compatible; like Gregory Clement, whose eyes were fixed only on material gain; like Alderman Foulkes, already committed too far to return to steadier ground; like Henry Marten, a convinced Republican. Thus the party was far from homogeneous.

Most of the Independent political party were, in religion, either Independent or more or less Separatist, while a few were dilettante radicals like Marten and the Challoners and therefore tolerant. Some were simply worldly profiteers who had jumped on the bandwaggon as soon as it was moving. Some, like Haselrig, were radical, Independent, and profiteers at once.

By contrast, not one member of Parliament of the Presbyterian party was a radical in religion. A few, like Strode and John Harrington, were genuine Presbyterians; but most were simply Puritans frightened of any loosening of the social system that toleration might permit, and apprehensive lest Independency might lead to the loss of their tithes. A layman wrote a strange and instructive pamphlet in 1645, 'A Letter of an Independent to Mr Glyn', stating that both groups were queer mixtures, but that the Independents feared the lack of toleration and the political potentialities of Presbyterianism.

If the King will give us liberty of conscience and not subjugate us to ecclesiastical power, we will submit ourselves to his civil power: and rather live with Episcopacy to establish monarchy than Presbytery to pull it down.

The fundamental Principle of this kingdom is that there should be a King and subjects.

Presbyterianism endangered this principle by putting the power of the Presbytery above that of the secular State.

Glyn, he said, was once an Independent like himself, but now he was for Presbytery.[1] That is, Glyn's change in politics was accompanied or preceded by a change in religion. His general outlook on the world made inevitable such a conversion. What is significant about this pamphlet is that it assumed the identification of religious

---

[1] 'The Letter of an Independent to Mr Glyn' (1645), Bodleian Library (Pamphlet 71).

and political parties as early as 1645. The changing of sides by Glyn, that most discreet of political opportunists, was still in some way connected with religion.

Classical Independency was not the platform for the really radical. The radical wing of the Independent party was on the whole closer to the non-Calvinist enthusiasm of the sects, but without being wedded to the separation of Church and State, for the radicals also were generally landowners. Radical Independency was found primarily in the Army. Cromwell and many of the other land-owning officers shared the same type of religious experience as the Leveller officers and the men of lesser rank. Consequently, religious radicals of all sorts were attracted to Cromwell's Army,[1] to the embarrassment of the 'pure' Independents.[2] With Cromwell's victories the prestige of the Independents increased enormously, for, though Cromwell never committed himself[3] to 'pure' Independency, he was looked upon as one of its leaders.[4] There was a close connexion between his Army Independents and the Independents in both Parliament and the Westminster Assembly. Three passages from Baillie are both illuminating and puzzling. Speaking of the slow progress of the Assembly, he remarked of the Independents in July 1644:

> Much is added to their pride and hopes by their service at the battle of York....The politick part in the Parliament is the stronger, who are resolute to conclude nothing in matters of Religion that may grieve the sectaries whom they count necessity for the time.[5]

He then said that the plot to remove Crawford and possibly Manchester from the Army was the means by which the Independents hoped to control the Army, 'to counterbalance us, to

---

[1] Baillie, *Letters and Journals*, II, 229.

[2] *Ibid.* p. 146.

[3] A common opinion is expressed in Hobbes's *Behemoth*: The various sects 'were Cromwell's best lords whereof he had a very great number in the Army and some in the House, whereof he himself was thought to be one, though in reality he was not steadily attracted to any one particular set, but applying himself always to the Faction that was strongest, was of a Colour like it' (in Maseres, *Tracts*, II, 586).

[4] Baillie, *Letters and Journals*, II, 153.   [5] *Ibid.* p. 211.

overawe the Assembly and Parliament both to their ends'.[1] He continued in the same letter:

While Cromwell is here, the House of Commons, without the least advertisement of any of us, or of the Assembly, passes an order, that the grand committee of both Houses, Assembly and us, shall consider of the means to unite us and the Independents; or if that be found impossible, to see how they may be tolerate...[And, he concluded bitterly] our greatest friends, Sir Henry Vane and the Solicitor, are the great procurers of all this.[2]

It seems clear that there was by 1644 a close link between the Independent divines, Cromwell and his Army, and 'the politick part in Parliament' under Vane and St John. But the precise nature of this link, and the identity of the supporters of Vane and St John, are not clear.[3] It would seem that the Independents were still a minority on the defensive, for as yet all they wanted was a safeguard against Presbyterian despotism, and they argued for toleration on the ground of expediency, that the support of the sects was necessary for military success.

Even by the end of 1644, I think it is true to say that the Independents were a composite party. The conservative Independents wanting decentralization of religion, being a minority, saw in Cromwell their potential saviour. The radical republicans, and those who had committed themselves so far that their necks were not safe without a decisive victory in the war, naturally supported the most ardent of the generals—Cromwell. Cromwell himself, wanting above all to safeguard the 'rights of religious experience', leaned towards the Independents as the party that would guarantee this.

Contemporaries agreed about the composite nature of the Independent party, though they rarely offered an intelligible explanation. Both Walker and Sir John Harris referred to the 'pure' and 'mixed' Independents, who feuded among themselves[4] and broke into innumerable divisions and subdivisions[5] although there remained

[1] *Ibid.* p. 230.   [2] *Ibid.*

[3] Baxter, *Reliquae Baxterianae*, I, 59, also refers to Vane's party in the House as supporters of and yet distinct from Cromwell's Army faction.

[4] Walker, *op. cit.* I, 75, and 'Sirrahnio' (Sir John Harris), *The Royal Quarrell*, 9 Feb. 1647–8.

[5] Walker, *op. cit.* II, 2.

two main groups, the Grandees, who collected the spoils, and the vulgar sort of Independents who would fare no better than the rest of the nation when the Grandees came to power.[1] Harris distinguished between Real and Royal Independents, possibly meaning by this that he equated the Republicans with the 'Real' Independents.

Clarendon made two incidental remarks which seem to throw light on a sociological division of importance. Referring to the Army confederates, who helped Cromwell to power, and not, as Mr Trevor-Roper suggests, to the whole Independent party, he noted with indignant surprise that scarce three of them 'at the beginning of the troubles were possessed of £300 land by the year',[2] yet referring to the whole party, or it may be only to its supporters in the City, he said of their struggle with the Presbyterians before Pride's Purge:

> The pulpit skirmishes were higher than ever: the Presbyterians in those fields losing nothing of their courage and having a notorious power in the City, notwithstanding the emulation of the Independents, who were more learned and rational; who though they had not such great congregations of the common people, infected and were followed by the most substantial and wealthy citizens and by others of better conditions; and to these men Cromwell and most of the Army officers adhered.... Liberty of conscience was now become the great charter.[3]

If Clarendon had so described the party after Pride's Purge, when many were anxious to cash in on the Revolution, then the two statements could be easily reconciled, but the latter remarks show that it appeared to him that the Independents had many influential backers. He, too, distinguished the Army Independents from the others, and like all other contemporaries, saw the matter of toleration as the cement of the alliance.

Clarendon's statements point to a sociological division in the party; Harris and Walker to a political one; while there is, as I have shown, also a religious division. Probably in most cases an Independent from the higher social strata would lean towards the conservative attitude in religion and politics, but this was by no means

---

[1] Walker, *op. cit.* I, 144.   [2] Clarendon, *History of the Rebellion*, XIV, § 26.
[3] *Ibid.* X, § 174. See also Hyde to Jermyn, 8 Jan. 1647 (quoted in B. H. G. Wormald, *Clarendon*, p. 187).

always the case. Vane and Pennington, two of the wealthier Independents, were religiously more radical; but, whereas Vane tended to be politically more conservative, and was absent at Pride's Purge and the King's trial, Pennington was not. Ireton took the more conservative attitude of classical Independency in religion and on social questions; yet circumstances forced both him and Cromwell, who was religiously more radical, to go to extreme political lengths. On the other hand, great landowners like Masham, Barrington and Armine were religiously and politically on the conservative wing, while on the radical religious and political wing were most of the Army officers, scarce any of whom 'were possessed of £300 land by the year'.

The Independents were a composite party, also, in that they combined all the radicals in different spheres together. There were the real radicals in religion, like Cromwell, who in politics was essentially conservative, 'not wedded or glued to any form', but wanting to rule like 'a village constable'. Lord Say and Sele was another case in point. Clarendon[1] described him as 'a man of a close and reserved nature, of a mean and narrow fortune, of great parts and of the highest ambition, but whose ambition would not be satisfied with offices and preferments without some condescensions and alterations in ecclesiastical matters. He had been for many years the oracle of those who were called puritans in the worst sense.' Say and Sele dropped out of affairs at Pride's Purge and did not improve his mean fortune. Other examples are Lord Wharton, conservative in politics but a consistent and radical religious Independent; and Alex Rigby, a conservative lawyer, but 'a desperate enemy of the Presbyterian Church', who, it is said, 'died after hearing a sermon on stewardship'.[2] Other 'lighter-headed Saints'[3] such as Ludlow, Thomas Scott, Cornelius Holland, and 'vainglorious, hare-brained Haselrig'[4] were radical in both politics and religion. Haselrig's Puritanism at times gave him qualms of conscience about 'the earthworm in his breast' when 'he espied a pleasant manor'.[5] He made a fortune from the lands of the Bishop

[1] Clarendon, *op. cit.* III, § 26.   [2] J. Vicars, *op. cit.*
[3] Walker, *op. cit.* II, 10.   [4] Somers, *Tracts*, VI, 921.
[5] 'Journal of Sir Roger Twisden', in *Archaeologia Cantana*, IV, 186. I am indebted to Mr Trevor-Roper for this reference.

of Durham and other Royalists, but remained consistently Republican, rejecting Cromwell's bait of a seat in the Upper House, for he would not 'take the bishop's seat because I know not how long after I shall keep the Bishop's lands'.[1]

Others were Republicans by principle, not merely by circumstance. Men like Marten, Harrington and Nevil were certainly not classical religious Independents, but were religious radicals in the sense that they wanted toleration. All Republicans were not Independents. Sir William Playters, 'one of Marten's gang', who was 'a great admirer and lover of handsome women and kept several',[2] managed in addition to be a Presbyterian elder,[3] and was excluded at Pride's Purge, after which he apparently took no further part in government. Algernon Sidney refused to take any part in the King's trial, and was wary of the Rump. Harrington in his diary wrote quite clearly as one not belonging to the Independents, and Henry Marten emphasized that Cromwell's followers were primarily for religious toleration, which was not his main concern. Thus the doctrinaire Republicans should not in one sense be identified with the Independents even though they probably all wanted toleration. Partly because of this common interest, and partly because events forced genuine Independents to be as radical as the Republicans, they were regarded as belonging to the one party. Yet Cromwell and his immediate supporters were only temporary Republicans, and many Independents, like Lord Say and Sele, would have nothing to do with Republicanism.

Some Independents were regarded as plain careerists, such as Mildmay, brought up at Charles' Court, 'and none', says Clarendon, 'more obsequious to the court while it flourished than he'; yet 'from the beginning of the parliament he concurred with those who were most violent against the court and like to prevail against it'.[4] Sir John Danvers was likewise of the Privy Chamber, the younger brother and heir of the Earl of Derby,

who, being neglected by his brother and having by a vain expense in his way of living contracted a vast debt, which he knew not how to pay, and being a proud formal weak man between seduced and a seducer, suffered

---

[1] Burton, *op. cit.* II, 423.   [2] Aubrey, *Brief Lives* (1949 ed.), p. 374.
[3] Shaw, *op. cit.* II, 426.   [4] Clarendon, *op. cit.* XI, § 237.

himself to be applied to their worst offices, taking it a high honour to sit upon the same bench with Cromwell, who employed and contemned him at once. Nor did that party of miscreants look upon any two men in the kingdom with more scorn and detestation as they did upon Danvers and Mildmay...[1]

Yet Mildmay in fact was a religious Independent, as was Whitelocke, who was always absent in the crises of his party, such as Pride's Purge, or the King's trial, and who, while the Independent Army was invading London in 1647 'was very busy about my own clients' causes, notwithstanding the many diversions and interruptions'.[2]

Any successful party has its fellow-travellers interested only in careers and profits, men such as the universally detested John Dove, an obscure alderman of Salisbury, who made a fortune from bishops' lands and offices, and Lord Howard of Escrick, whose financial immorality became too much even for the Rump. And of course, there was Speaker Lenthall who 'told the Officers of the Army and Members who came to invite him to sit again May 6th [1659] that he had a soul to save, and that he was not satisfied in point of law, conscience or prudence that they could sit again. But at last when he considered he had an estate to save (as he told another friend) that over-balanced all his former objections'.[3]

Clement Walker, disgruntled since his ejection from Parliament at Pride's Purge, labelled the whole party as careerists, monopolizing all the rich employments. 'They give daily to one another for pretended Services, Arrears, and Losses, great sums of money; many of their Largesses I have already set down' (taking most of his book for the setting). '...All the cheating, covetous, ambitious persons of the Land, are united together under the name and title of The Godly, the Saints, etc.'[4] To some, undoubtedly, the Independent chariot was a heaven sent band-waggon.

The creation of the party cannot, however, be explained by whatever it did when corrupted with power, or by the statement that it included a number of careerists, especially in view of the fact that

---

[1] *Ibid.*　　　　　　　　　　[2] *Memorials* (1853 ed.), III, 187.
[3] William Prynne, *Conscientious Serious Theological and Legal Quaeres*, p. 48. See also Ludlow, *Memoirs*, II, 78.
[4] Walker, *op. cit.* I, 143.

the Rump Republicans became the enemies of Oliver Cromwell, and thus lost their offices. Walker of course attributed the hatching of this deep plot to Cromwell who used the power politics of the Turk and 'jugled the States sword into the Independent scabbard'.[1] To Walker he was nothing but a bloodthirsty self-seeking Machiavel: 'Oliver is a Bird of Prey, you may know by his Bloody Beak.'[2]

If it had been a scheme from the beginning, it was indeed a deep plot. It was too deep for Henry Marten, who, when he saw Walker's *History*, jotted down a brief rejoinder:

> It is clear to me that a whole Parliament can have no plot at all: they are so numerous and so mingled in temper and education, age and interests, that so great a party as he calls Independents could not drive on any project of that bulk, so long abrewing, with secrecy sufficient for such an enterprise. And it is not clear to me that the single person you speak of did lay those eggs, or sett a brood upon them which we see hatched indeed to his advantage. He was a man of high spirit from the beginning, very active and vigilant: he had got a crew about him of blades that would follow him through any other fire to avoid the fire of persequitions.[3]

As Marten himself was far from being one of Cromwell's blades, this is significant.

The party was seen to be composite by contemporaries. Baxter, writing of Pride's Purge, said, 'And thus when the two parts of the House were ejected and imprisoned, this third part [i.e. the Independents] composed of the Vanists, the Independents, and other Sects, with the Democratical Party, was left by Cromwell to do his business....'[4] This acute observation makes a number of important distinctions in the party—the Republicans (the democratical party), the conservative Independents (the Independents), and the radical Independents (the other sects). In that case who were the Vanists? Are we to assume that they were the upper gentry? These varying groups were held together by a radicalism that always included a religious radicalism, for as Walker said, the Independents religiously were 'mere enthusiastiques, of a speculative and high flying religion, too high for earth, and too low for heaven'.[5]

[1] Walker, *op. cit.* I, 28.   [2] *Ibid.* II, 104.
[3] Historical Manuscripts Commission, *Thirteenth Report*, Appendix IV. MS. of Captain Loder Symonds, 400.
[4] Baxter, *Reliquae Baxterianae*, I, 63.   [5] Walker, *op. cit.* I, 28.

The history of their rise to power illustrates both their divisions and their underlying religious unity, and also a basic social unity, for, though differing in degree, they were all gentry. Being gentry, they not only very frequently held the advowsons and tithes of the parish church, but they combined with the parson on the local level to represent the intimate Church-State relationship which most people, both radical and conservative, saw to be of the very nature of society. Harrington wrote: 'Where civil liberty is entire, it includes liberty of conscience; where liberty of conscience is entire, it includes civil liberty',[1] a remark which presupposes the same close Church-State relationship that Laud believed in. Few gentry would accept Roger Williams' logic of complete Church-State separation, even if they were sympathetic to other parts of his theology, for the whole social structure was involved, as well as the consideration of tithes. The gentry might hate the Laudian Church's centralized interference in social and religious matters; they might fear a similar power if Presbyterianism were firmly established, but they would consider the Separatist solution socially and theologically untenable. Independency would seem the solution, and not only for the religiously minded among them, for the man indifferent to personal piety might in the seventeenth century be more concerned than the other-worldly religious man over ecclesiastical change because it would upset the social milieu, to which the latter was comparatively indifferent.

THE INDEPENDENT CONGREGATIONS

The history of the Independents shows that though the gentry of the party—and it was almost entirely a party of gentry—differed in outlook and social status, nevertheless there was an underlying unity of religion which connected them with the Independent churches. And indeed the Independent churchmen did not mind very much which section of the party was in power, the Rumpers, the Cromwellians or even the Fifth Monarchists (though the latter were not really an Independent group), as long as it was pro-Independent. The connexion between the Independent churches and the various

[1] Quoted in Woodhouse, *op. cit.* Introduction, p. 82.

groups of political Independents suggests that the theology of Independency did affect the world view of the Independents in the Parliament and Army. Hugh Peters, as shown, was involved with the London radicals in 1642; Vane was linked with Nye and Goodwin by the Royalists as early as 1643; and similar associations continued. Thomas Goodwin defended Pride's Purge-in 'Right and Might Well Met'.[1] Peters, 'Chaplain in Ordinary to two great Potentates, Lucifer and Oliver',[2] was the inseparable companion of the Regicides, bolstering up their courage with sermons based on such appropriate texts as 'Let the praise of God be in their mouths and a two-edged sword in their hands', while an earlier sermon: 'Bind your kings in chains', dripped blood. Other Independents, like Thomas Scott of Canterbury, possibly a relation of the member of Parliament, circulated petitions urging the King's death.[3]

The part played by the Independent congregations was indicated in an Independent pamphlet of 1660[4] in which the writer concluded that God's present judgment came upon them because they had acquiesced in the political radicalism of the Army. In 1648, he said, Presbyterians and Episcopalians had pointed out their errors. 'Yet among ourselves I do not find any dissent or discussion from them published to the world by any of our congregational party: but rather such books that did justify and approve the same.'

He continued that the only Independent who had spoken against this radicalism at the time, William Sedgwick, had soon changed his opinion in his 'A New View of the Army Remonstrance'. He then enumerated the evil actions of the radicals in destroying the monarchy, purging Parliament and abolishing the Lords, and blamed not only the Army but also the churches: 'Which of our gathered churches declared the trouble of our hearts and the great dislike of the Army's disobedience to the authority of the Lords and Commons that raised them?' They had 'not only wished the Army

[1] Woodhouse, *op. cit.* p. 212.   [2] Walker, *op cit.* II, 179.

[3] *Congregational Hist. Soc. Trans.* VII, 264. According to Walker, *op. cit.* II., 116, Nye, together with radical London aldermen Foulkes, Gybs, Woolaston, etc., petitioned against peace with the King.

[4] 'The Moderate Independent Proposing a Word in Season to the Gathered Churches', by Salem Philalathes (London, 1660).

God's speed, and so are partakers of all their evil deeds, but have joined with them and owned them in all those woeful Revolutions'.

They had supported the Rump, Cromwell, the Restored Rump,[1] those 'last sediments of the House of Commons', and finally Colonel Lambert. 'For our present unhappy position we should judge and condemn ourselves.'[2]

The Independent congregations had played a definite part in the affairs of the Commonwealth and Protectorate. Apparently there had been some kind of organization among the various churches, for when Lilburne held a conference to discuss the proposed constitution, there were four representatives from the London Independents (not members of Parliament) as well as four from the Army, four Levellers and four Republican members of Parliament,[3] which suggests that there must have been some kind of Independent non-parliamentary organization that was loosely linked with the Army and the political party.

The Commonwealth and Protectorate governments made great use of the Independent ministers. Owen, Nye and Peters acted as if they were government officials,[4] while the Independent and Baptist congregations (or, more likely, perhaps, a few prominent ministers) virtually nominated the Barebones' Parliament.[5] Independency was almost the established Church—but not quite. The sect-type Christianity of the Army and poorer classes, although not strong enough of itself to abolish tithes, did prevent Independency from reaching that logical development. Its spirit had infected the leading Independent, Cromwell himself, even though he finally withdrew from his allegiance to the Saints, through the powerful influence of his friends among the conservative gentry and officers—

[1] Ludlow and John Owen consulted to draw up a list of surviving Rumpers (Ludlow, *op. cit.* II, 74).

[2] 'The Moderate Independent.'

[3] Lilburne, *History of the Second Agreement* (quoted in Woodhouse, *op. cit.* pp. 347–8).

[4] *Thurloe State Papers*, III, 281. Notice how active the Independent congregations and ministers were just before the Restoration and how the Army leaders sought their advice (*Clarke Papers*, IV, 81, 184).

[5] *Thurloe State Papers*, I, 395, and S. R. Gardiner, *History of the Commonwealth and Protectorate*, II, 276.

5-2

and in so doing took over Charles' position as the antichrist. Just before his death, with the calling of the Savoy Conference, he seemed to be moving in the direction of establishing Independency, but it is not certain that he would have done so.

THE ARMY INDEPENDENTS

When the Independents captured the Army command in 1644, it looked as if they had gained all, but when this frightened their less radical supporters into siding with the Presbyterians, control of Parliament was lost, and the Army wing of the party of necessity became the more important. The salvation of the Presbyterians in Parliament depended on getting rid of the Army. When troops were needed for Ireland in 1647, Hollis threw away an opportunity, for Parliament refused to satisfy the demands of the Army for arrears of pay and an indemnity. This refusal united the rank and file Levellers with the Army Independent leaders. The leaders of the Levellers, at any rate, were all Separatists in religion, and therefore were united also with the Independents, and with Cromwell especially, on the question of toleration. And so the Army became a vital political force, demanding, as they were 'no mere mercenary army', a say in the final settlement of the kingdom. The Levellers naturally used the opportunity to push their demands for democracy based on the sovereignty of the people, and the Independent officers, alarmed equally by the radical Levellers and the conservative Presbyterians, were forced to undertake the making of a political constitution. Their programme, 'The Heads of the Proposals', seems to be in the nature of an alternative to Leveller demands rather than a party platform considered and worked for since the war began. It contained clauses which, if carried out, would alleviate the burdens and grievances of lesser gentry, and at the same time protect property rights from Leveller encroachments. The Court of Wards was attacked, but compensation was to be paid. The 'troublesome and contentious' question of tithes was to be considered, but there was no promise of their abolition. Legal procedure was to be reformed. Disposal of the great offices of state for the next ten years was to be vested in both Houses of Parliament. Apart from clauses abolishing the power of ecclesiastical officers, and virtually ensuring toleration, the bulk of the programme was concerned almost entirely with devising machinery that would make impossible a return to non-parliamentary government. But it was not democratic. There was to be decentralization of borough seats, but the representation was to be based not on population, but on rates, which would give London a very big representation, for after a century and a half of centralization of trade, London was far more wealthy proportionately per head of population than any other town.[1]

To get another army of their own, Holles and the Presbyterians gave the London militia back to the control of the City. The Independents took fright and fled to the Army. From that time until the setting up of the Republic, the Army wing of the Independents dominated the party, for the Parliamentary Independents practically ceased to count, and, if they refused to co-operate with the Army, were discarded, like Lord Say and his sons, at Pride's Purge.[2]

Those Independents that fled to the Army were presumably leading ones. Three lists of them survive, all containing fifty-eight names. Those in Rushworth[3] and the Lords' Journal[4] are almost identical; those in Percival's list[5] vary, containing twenty-four alternative names. Most of these are future Rumpers, but with the exception of Harrison, Cromwell, Ireton, Morley and the two Salways, are the less radical members of the Rump.

The Army then marched on London. Some of the suburbs, such

---

[1] Even in 1523 London was probably twice as wealthy per head of population as Norwich, the second city of the kingdom. Its population was possibly fifty thousand, five times as great as that of Norwich, but its tax assessment was ten times as great. And much the same ratio of wealth existed between London and the other provincial cities, with the exception of some of the Suffolk wool villages. Long Melford and Lavenham both had a much higher *per capita* assessment than even London. (I owe most of this information to Dr W. G. Hoskins.)

[2] *D.N.B.*, and C. H. Firth, *op. cit.* p. 231.

[3] Rushworth, *Historical Collections*, IV, 755.

[4] *Lords' Journal*, IX, 385. Rushworth has Capt. James Scott, Crowder, Bosville and Livesey, and omits Purefoy, Hutchinson, Lenthall and Rowland Wilson who are in the Lords' list.

[5] Historical Manuscripts Commission. Egmont MSS., I, 440.

as Southwark,[1] went over to the Independents, and enabled them to gain the City without difficulty. This defection of a large section of London would suggest a sizeable Independent—or more likely, Independent and Leveller—faction within the stronghold of Presbyterianism.

The Army then partially purged Parliament. By force the Independents had gained control of Parliament, the City, and the King—and also had taken over the Presbyterian policy of trying to come to terms with him.[2] This policy ruptured their alliance with the Levellers, which was cemented again only by the outbreak of the second Civil War. At the momentous Prayer Meeting at Windsor, the officers took over the Republicanism of the Levellers and determined to bring to account 'Charles Stuart, that man of blood'.[3] Having defeated the Scots at Preston in October 1648, they marched on London with the Levellers, sharing a common programme based on the sovereignty of the people. The pro-Independent newspaper, the *Moderate*, said, 'If God hath ordained all things in heaven and earth for the good of the people, what earthly principalities or powers, which the people hath chosen for their good, can enjoin them to obedience in things destructive and unlawful?'[4] But when again they seized Parliamentary power, at Pride's Purge on 6 December 1648, the Independents repudiated this radical political theory of the Levellers. In the Army debate at Whitehall they also repudiated Separatism, the radical religious theory of the Levellers.

THE ARMY DEBATES AT WHITEHALL, 1648[5]

Cromwell, religious radical and social conservative, found in Independency the mean between the two. Ireton, the theoretician of the Independents, integrated his religion and his social theory. His ideal for society was embodied in the decentralized Calvinism that retained the vital connexion between Church and State, which was in essence the classical Independency of the Dissenting Brethren

---

[1] Whitelocke, *Memorials*, II, 189, and Clarendon, *op. cit.* x, § 111.
[2] I owe this observation to Mr Trevor-Roper.
[3] Gardiner, *History of the Great Civil War*, IV, 118 ff.
[4] 13 Oct. 1648.   [5] Reprinted in Woodhouse, *op. cit.* pp. 125–78.

worked out in theory in 1643. He expressed his views in the significant Whitehall Debates which took place in December 1648, a few days after Pride's Purge. They were based on the discussion of the religious clause in Lilburne's 'Agreement of the People' by Army Grandees and Leveller Agitators.

The Independents, with the help of the Army radicals, were finally in control of Parliament, and now had to govern. Their religious attitude was of vital importance—Independency or Separatism. Ostensibly the debate was over Lilburne's clause for toleration; it was in fact over Church-State relationships. The Independents wanted the relationship retained, with a religious toleration that would not endanger the State. The Levellers declared that religious toleration was logically impossible unless Church and State were separate. Liberty of conscience 'is preferred by us before life',[1] said Overton; it was essential that the magistrate be given no power whatsoever in religion; Church and State must therefore be separated.

Throughout the debate Ireton stressed the fact that he was genuinely concerned with religious toleration, but was not sure that, having it completely, anarchy could be prevented:

...Any man submitting to the civil government of the nation should have liberty to serve God according to his conscience. This is a right, I will agree to that. That is not the question amongst us. For if that were the question, I should be sure to give my *no* to the allowance of any man to be punished for his conscience, and if I had a thousand noes in one I should give it, and that as loud as any man....

But here's the case. The question is now: Whether you shall make such a provision for men that are conscientious in order that they may serve God according to their light and conscience, as shall necessarily debar any kind of restraint on anything that any man will call religion?...though they were to practise idolatry, to practise atheism and anything that is against the light of God.[2]

The seemingly involved debate hinged on this question, whether Church and State should be separate. Three main arguments were advanced.

The Independent Grandees said that the magistrate could bind men's bodies, but not their consciences,[3] equating the sphere of

---

[1] *Ibid.* p. 139.   [2] *Ibid.* p. 143.   [3] *Ibid.* p. 130.

grace, where they wanted toleration, with man's soul, and with his body the sphere of nature, where they did not. Overton repudiated this as a spurious distinction. If a magistrate 'hath power over my body, he hath power to keep me at home when I should go abroad to serve God'.[1]

Then the Independents argued that the Jewish magistrates of the Old Testament were the pattern for the State as well as for the Church, when they were commanded to ensure the observance of the rules of behaviour. Ireton pointed out that their power had extended to those outside Israel, and therefore should be applied to those outside the Church now.

They were commanded to beat down the idols and groves and images of the land whither they went; they were commanded that they should not suffer the stranger that was within the gate to work on the sabbath...they did it considered as civil magistrates...and not as ecclesiastical magistrates or as persons signifying or typifying the power of ecclesiastical officers under the Gospel; and therefore what was a rule of duty to them (unless men can show me a ground of change) should be a rule and duty of magistrates now.[2]

The Levellers held that God had chosen Israel to be a pattern for the Church only and not for the State, and because of this, He had chosen the magistrates to keep Israel especially pure.[3]

The third main argument arose over the scope of the magistrate's power. Did it embrace all the Ten Commandments, or was it limited to the last six concerning the relationships between man and man? Nye, the Independent minister, said that as God punishes a people for its sin, and the greatest sin is idolatry, for their own good the people should grant the magistrate power to enforce religious laws.[4] Collier, 'a great mechanical dipper', speaking for the Levellers, said that when the gospel abrogated Jewish judicial law, excommunication in the New Testament replaced the death penalty of the Old Testament for idolatry and adultery. Ireton and Hewson held that 'that which was evil then remains upon the same grounds

---

[1] Woodhouse, *op. cit.* p. 139.   [2] *Ibid.* pp. 155–6.
[3] *Ibid.* p. 158. Here John Goodwin, that very heretical Independent, argued for the Separatists.
[4] *Ibid.* p. 160.

equally evil now' and therefore the Christian magistrate should restrain all signs of it, even as the Jewish magistrates had.[1]

These debates showed clearly that the Independents were no Brownists or Separatists. Beside their genuine desire for religious toleration, they also (in Ireton's words) 'would have an eye to property', and valued most highly the preserving of human society in peace;[2] therefore they feared the consequences of irreligious anarchy. They were bound to the Separatists by the value they placed on religious experience and shared their method of argument from Scripture. They did not want the godly persecuted.

The Separatists wanted toleration in the sphere of nature, although many were most intolerant within their own sects, the 'sphere of grace'. The Independents wanted toleration in the sphere of grace, but feared its consequences in the sphere of nature. Almost without exception the Presbyterian attacks on the Independents condemned their tolerance. Much of this was the equivalent of twentieth-century political tactics, but it cannot be dismissed as being based entirely on political expediency, for if their language did not reveal a passionate religious controversy, what language could possibly do so? ('I will tell you what this Independency is: It is the genus generalissimum of all errors, heresies, blasphemies and schisms...a composition of Jew, Christian and Turk.'[3])

Because the organization of the Church was an essential part of seventeenth-century society, the difference cannot be classified as purely political or purely religious. Who would advocate the dangerous experiment of the Independents, so near that of the Separatists, unless they were really concerned about toleration?

THE INDEPENDENTS IN POWER

When the Independents came to power at Pride's Purge, although the constitutional and social programmes of the different groups among them varied, all of them advocated and permitted a very real degree of religious toleration, though they never separated Church and State, nor abolished the hated tithes as urged by their former allies, the Separatists. Such measures proved too much for

[1] *Ibid.* pp. 165–8.   [2] *Ibid.* p. 130.   [3] Walker, *op. cit.* p. 27.

even the Parliament of Saints, and Cromwell, of all the Independents
the most sympathetic to the sects, in December 1653 took the part of
the conservatives in that Parliament, and ousted the Fifth Monarchists
rather than embark on their radical programme. As the Fifth
Monarchists saw, the issue was quite decisive. 'Lord,' cried their
angry leader, Vavasor Powell, 'have our Army men all apostasised
from their principles! What is become of all declarations, pro-
testations and professions? Are they choked with lands, parks and
manors? Let us go home and say "Lord, wilt thou have Oliver
Cromwell or Jesus Christ to reign over us?".'[1]

Except for this brief interlude of the Saints' Parliament, controlled
by Separatists rather than Independents, there was no attempt to go
the way of the Separatists in Church-State relationships. Neither
the Republic nor the Protectorate Parliaments, nor the rule of the
Major-Generals, upset the pattern of a decentralized Calvinist Church
organization, the Puritan-Anglican Church without bishops.

Except for the fact that it was a Republic and there was toleration,
did the rule of the Rump differ in any essentials from that of the
Presbyterians? After the radical events of 1648-9, the effective
leadership of Parliament was not apparently with the lesser gentry,
for the Army leaders were busily occupied in Scotland and Ireland,
and Haselrig, Vane and St John could hardly be said to represent
them. Was there any attempt at decentralization? There was little
fear of the Republic ruining London's trade, judging by the praise
for the Republic of the Independent Slingsby Bethel, the great
London financier, who 'kept no house but lived upon chops', made
his contribution to seventeenth-century literature with 'The World's
Mistake in Oliver Cromwell', and spoke about the late king's death
'in very indecent terms'.[2]

The Rump was an oligarchy with no positive policy except that
of self-interest. Corrupted by privilege and possession, it did not
see the necessity for the semblance of democracy to satisfy the Army,
nor for righteousness to satisfy *the* Independent, Cromwell.

With Cromwell in power, a new factor emerged. The Independents, Walker complained, had always built up their membership
from family circles. In Parliament 'they come in couples more than

[1] *Calendar of State Papers, Domestic*, 1653-4, p. 304.　　[2] *D.N.B.*

unclean Beasts to the Ark'.[1] Cromwell had a ramifying tribe of friends and relations on whom he could generally count for support in Parliament, and in the politics of the Protectorate family ties were always a factor that could cut across other considerations. As Mr Trevor-Roper has pointed out, such a new Court, with new offices, was not better than the old to the radical Independents.

One seems forced to the conclusion that there was no real Independent policy. The party came together for a variety of reasons; religious toleration, which eventually became the official slogan of the party, may not have been the strongest tie. With the Rump, Republicanism became the official political creed. Hatred of the old Court with its offices, which hurt the pride and pocket of many lesser gentlemen, and, inevitably, personal grievances, all played their part.

Once the party was in active existence, like any political party, its aims were often obscured in the struggle for place and power, and in gaining preferments for friends and relatives. The moral decline of the party after it seized power at Pride's Purge is theologically as well as historically instructive. Not only were its obligations to the Levellers repudiated, not only was a new class of London speculators created in the orgy of land speculations which financed the Rump,[2] but the common soldiers were swindled of their pay by the system of debentures.[3] Meanwhile, many leading Independents made fortunes through the money committees of the Rump and through buying up lands by 'doubling', a 'singular invention' for getting rid of a hot asset suggested by a leading Presbyterian divine, the ingenious Dr Burgess.[4] Bulstrode Whitelocke's *Memorials* are rendered no less dull by the continual notes of handouts for party supporters. When the leaders of the party themselves began indulging in an orgy of money-making and self-seeking, it could hardly expect to retain the support of any Army benefiting little from its rule and imbued with the straitening ethical ideals of Puritan Christianity. But even the Army, when in power during the years of anarchy 1658–60, showed no vestige of

[1] Walker, *op. cit.* I, 173.
[2] H. E. Chesney, *Royal Historical Society Trans.* (1932), pp. 181 ff.
[3] C. Hill, *English Historical Review* (1940), p. 238.
[4] Baillie, *Letters and Journals*, II, 411.

any policy except trying to prevent the Restoration. Although all-powerful, it was very unpopular. A Londoner wrote in December 1659: 'The soldiers here are so vilified, scorned and hissed that they are ashamed to march, and many officers, when they go into the City, dare not even wear their swords for fear of affront. And thus God has blasted them and they become vile in the eyes of the people.'[1]

[1] Tanner, *Constitutional Conflicts of the Seventeenth Century*, p. 211.

CHAPTER V

A Universal Chaos?

ON the evidence collected, it is difficult indeed to make any generalized statements about the Independent party, except that its early leaders and its later radical supporters, the Regicides, were Independents or favourers of toleration in religion, and were often Republicans.

It is probable that there remains vital evidence to be found on this subject; if not, then it is most significant that in a situation where one might expect a sociological pattern to emerge it does not. I am indeed attracted by Mr Trevor-Roper's hypothesis[1] that in essence the Independents were the lesser gentry, but even this needs most important qualifications.

It is the function—or perhaps the fate—of general statements about historical periods to be broken down into smaller statements, and to stimulate investigation which may modify or even overthrow them. The generalization of the Marxist historians that the Civil War was a class war is no exception. This general statement has been broken down into particular classifications of the different types among the classes taking part, but these classifications themselves need further investigation.

The Independents were a composite group, which in its early stages probably revolved around a few dominant members of Parliament who felt strongly about Church government and toleration. The number of these religiously radical members was at least fifty-seven—the number of those who in 1647 voted for the laity being allowed to expound the Bible.[2] The minimum number of Republicans can also be fixed at thirty-four by the vote of 1647 when Henry Marten moved no further addresses to the King,[3] which,

---

[1] 'The Gentry, 1540–1640', *Economic History Review* Supplement (1953).

[2] *Commons Journals*, v, 34.

[3] *Ibid.* v, 312. Most Republicans were Independents, but some apparently were not, e.g. Sir William Playters. See above, p. 62.

significantly, was opposed by Cromwell and Sir John Evelyn of Wiltshire. The total following of the Independents in the House in January 1648 would be no less than 141,[1] although the real core of the party was most likely to be those fifty-eight who fled to the Army in 1647 and the Army officers who received them. Though 209 members appear to have given some kind of allegiance to the Rump, many were obviously very half-hearted—notice the small attendances—and many more were apparent careerists, following whichever party was most likely to hold the power.

The real core of the party, however, consisted of religiously strong Independents who, at an early stage, ventured much for it—men such as Vane, Say and Sele, Haselrig, Cromwell and Lord Brooke, with active support from men like Sir William Armine. All these influential men either had or built up strong support from lesser figures, and in this resembled the dominating figures of eighteenth-century politics, except that they took religion very seriously. Vane had followers like the Salways; Haselrig controlled Blackston; Armine the Lincolnshire group; and Say and Sele and Lord Brooke had a very wide influence. Cromwell, of course, dominated the Army faction in Parliament. All these leading figures were strong Independents. Those who followed them may sometimes have done so because of religious conviction, but often their support may have been for some other motive, and on the religious issues they might merely follow their patron from loyalty or expediency. This could explain the sizeable percentage of non-Independent political Independents, and also partly account for the big percentage of lesser gentry, clients of their more influential fellows, though this factor would also be present in the Presbyterian and Royalist parties.

In 1640 the zealous Puritans wanted to abolish episcopacy, but had no further defined ambitions. Very few indeed had thought of the decentralized Calvinist system of Independency. They did not turn to this until they had bought Scottish aid with the hated Covenant. And then Independency in practice was not like the iron-bound system of New England. What was it indeed but Puritan Anglicanism without those wretched, interfering, persecuting bishops! Not Separatism, that would break the parish

[1] Brunton and Pennington, *Members of the Long Parliament*, p. 38.

government machinery by which the gentry upheld their social position. No tithes abolished, for these valued property rights were even more important to the lesser gentry than to the greater, for they were an appreciable part of their incomes. But with the gentry as patrons of autonomous parish churches, it would indeed be a 'happy bishopless Eden' for the gentry. The Independent type of church organization preserved the social structure of the Church of England for the gentry in the sphere of local politics, in no way led to social anarchy nor endangered property,[1] and yet abolished the not inconsiderable religious and social opposition of the anti-Puritan bishops.

But would not a 'lame Erastian presbytery' controlled by the Long Parliament suit the convenience of the Independents just as well? Or, to put the case in another way, would not an Independent system suit the Presbyterian members of Parliament just as well? If religion was a thing indifferent to them, surely the answer must be 'yes'. I can only conclude that the Independent leaders were genuinely afraid of religious intolerance, and that the Presbyterians were genuinely apprehensive about the religious anarchy that might follow the decentralization of the Church. In this period, religious and secular motives were so closely connected that observers cannot arbitrarily set the frontiers. It is often difficult to tell, for instance, whether the vituperative Walker is vilifying his opponents for their theology or their politics.

In the Independents' fight for religious toleration, they had to become more radical than they would have wished, and came into alliance with Republicans on the one hand (who in any case, often wanted toleration, and were mostly gentry) and with the Army Levellers on the other. Clarendon saw their dilemma in January 1647:

...to think that those who have good fortunes and excellent understandings, have a design to dissolve monarchy and change the government which would carry away with it so much of the common law, as would shake

---

[1] Notice how in the Putney Debates, between the Levellers and the Independents, the main emphasis of the latter is on the preservation of property and society in peace (Woodhouse, *Puritanism and Liberty*, pp. 1–124, particularly pp. 53 ff.).

their own property and every part of their condition, which made life pleasant to them, or that they are not themselves now more afraid of the people than ever they pretended to be of tyranny, is such an independency upon reason, as I believe no Independent of either House is guilty of, though they have no other way of keeping up their party than by conniving at all licence and opinion of equality which yet they restrain as far as is necessary to their business in hand.[1]

In the Army, Republicanism and Independency fused, especially after the second Civil War of 1648, when Cromwell and Ireton adopted Republicanism simply because they could not trust the King. Then, while the civilian Independents of the House were temporarily unimportant, many withdrawing, the Army, particularly the Army officer members of Parliament, dominated the scene. It is here that Mr Trevor-Roper's thesis is most illuminating, if it is applied to the Army officer Independents, who were lesser gentry and put forward the demands of that class most consistently. Cromwell, Ireton, Ludlow, Whalley, Desborough and their like were all lesser gentry, opposed to the Levellers on the one hand and the Court gentry on the other, but united with the other sections of Independent gentry by the common demand for religious toleration.

Their opponents always—I have found no exception—attacked the Independents for approving religious toleration. There were gradations even in the radical religious outlook shared to some extent by every group in the party, as shown in the Army Debates at White-hall, and again in the debate over Naylor the self-proclaimed Messiah in the first Protectorate Parliament.[2] One group, wanting a complete toleration on the Separatist model, was only divided from the Leveller-sectaries by sociological considerations. These same considerations partly accounted for the desire of the other group to retain the existing local church system and to limit its toleration to what it would define as the genuinely religious sphere. This group consisted on the whole of the lesser Independent gentry, although Cromwell took the more radical position shared by near-

[1] Hyde to Jermyn, 8 Jan. 1647 (quoted in B. H. G. Wormald, *Clarendon*, p. 187).
[2] See Burton, *Parliamentary Diary*, I, 24 ff. The majority of Independents wished to execute Naylor for blasphemy.

Leveller Independents on the one hand and the high and mighty, such
as Vane and Pennington, on the other. But within these two limits
there was a demand for a genuine type of religious toleration.

In brief then, it seems certain that religion was a basic factor that
bound together this heterogeneous Independent party; that it was
a composite party, politically, socially, and even religiously; that the
conservative members of the party, though desiring a limited toleration and Independent church government, wished to retain the close
relationship between Church and State, especially on the parochial
level, and for this reason, and not, as Hexter suggests, for reasons
of politics, some of them became temporarily Presbyterian elders.
But events forced them to side with the radicals who were genuine
Republicans and wanted complete religious toleration (though
sometimes, as in the case of Cromwell, a radical demand for toleration was combined with a political conservatism). I think it probable
that the Army wing of the party did in fact represent to a large
extent the aspirations of the lesser gentry, but like all parliamentary
parties of the time, the parliamentary wing displayed a pyramid-like
social structure, and its leaders were not lesser gentry. I can see little
consistency in their programme except a desire to win the war and
to gain a degree of toleration. These aims alone united the party.
All other aims were sought by sections only of the group. I would
suggest that the ultimate answer to the social problem here lies in
allegiances to smaller personal loyalties in each local sphere, to small
groups of politicians who controlled the social status and political
advancement of their less influential followers.

I am by no means satisfied that what I have said completely solves
this perplexing problem, but it seems to me from the evidence
I have found that a clear-cut class struggle on Marxist lines does not
emerge in a study of the main protagonists of the Civil War,
although a class division is apparent between the Levellers and the
Independent Grandees. The Civil War was primarily a war among
the gentry, and each of the three factions was composed of greater,
court, lesser and country gentry, of London and country merchants.
Economic and social motives are clearly present, but the Marxist
division between old feudal classes and the *bourgeoisie* is false,
although it gives some illumination, and so, too, is the analysis of

Mr Trevor-Roper into greater and lesser gentry, which gives more light. For in the first half of the seventeenth century, at any rate, the countless number of economic and social pressure groups acted in and were occasioned by the much smaller setting of local personal loyalties. The Independent party was not one great doctrinaire party, but a large number of small groups often owing allegiance to local patrons, and these groups were loosely united by circumstances or religion. Religion, which in the seventeenth century was an essential factor, was frequently a negative influence. Men knew what they disliked or feared, or were allied to a group whose leader's attitude in religion they had to follow. Consequently the Independent party has no clear-cut social aims, nor is it the mouthpiece of one class, even though economic and social factors are clearly present. Each party had its great patrons with their bands of followers. They differ sociologically only in so far as each has one distinctive centre of power, which, though by no means all-embracing, tends to send each party in a different direction. The Royalists follow the Court and Anglicanism; the Presbyterians, London and centralized Calvinism; the Independents, the Army and decentralized Calvinism.

At present I think little more can with safety be said. Like the first *History of Independency* this study has largely negative conclusions. Certain limits to the chaos perhaps have been set, but many problems remain:

> When I consider the intricacy of this my undertaking, how perplexed it is, how intangled with various changings, counterchangings, revolutions, revoltings, and betrayings of Parties,...how full of divisions, and sub-divisions; insomuch that they who are Friends and hold together in one Interest or Faction, are Opposites in another. Methinks my labour is as vain as his that attempted to take the picture of Proteus.... What Historian can find a method in so universal a Chaos?[1]

[1] Walker, *op. cit.* II, 2.

APPENDIX A

Detailed list of party supporters with statistical analysis

THE following list includes all the important members of Parliament, and most of the others, who were not excluded by Pride's Purge or who later made their peace with the Rump; all who fled to the Army in 1647 during the temporary Presbyterian triumph in Parliament; all who signed Charles' death warrant;[1] and a few others, active in the Barebones' or Protectorate Parliaments, who appear to have been Independents.

It is intended to be a convenient summary for students away from source material, and a basis for any who may embark on the subject on a larger scale. As far as the religious affiliation of the members goes, it pioneers some new ground.

Under each name is listed his constituency and the year in which he entered the Long Parliament, if he did so, in order that Recruiters may easily be identified.

First it is noted whether the person fled to the Army in 1647, that is, whether he was an early Independent in the times when their success was doubtful. The information is from Rushworth[2] except when it is specifically stated to come from Percival's list.[3]

Any part taken in the King's trial is noted, and then (from Brunton and Pennington) any part in the Rump Parliament, with any subsequent Parliamentary activity, known with reasonable certainty, up to the death of Cromwell.

Then follows a very brief résumé of family background, education and social importance, which may be of some use until histories of all the seventeenth-century Parliaments appear.[4] When other

---

[1] In Gardiner, *History of the Great Civil War*, IV, 309.
[2] *Historical Collections*, VII, 755.   [3] H.M.C. Egmont MSS., I, 440.
[4] Miss M. F. Keeler's *The Long Parliament, 1640–1641*, came out just as this was going to Press. She gives admirable sketches of most of the original members of the Long Parliament, and makes my notes on those members,

references are not given, the sources used have been: the *Dictionary of National Biography*, not altogether a satisfactory source for this type of work; the *Manuscript* of W. D. Pink in the John Rylands Library, Manchester, which although undocumented, has all the signs of care and thoroughness; J. and J. A. Venn's brief biographical notes in their *Alumni Cantabrigienses*; and Miss C. V. Wedgwood's excellent brief notes now at the Institute of Historical Research, London, which filled in some important gaps. Purchasers of bishops' land are taken from the original list of buyers in Rawlinson MSS. B 239, Bodleian Library.

Finally, the scanty evidence I have regarding their religious attitudes is set out, coming mainly from A. G. Matthews' monumental work, *Calamy Revised* (abbreviated in references to *C.R.*), which is arranged alphabetically, and, except where otherwise stated, the reference in the work is to the minister's name mentioned. Dr G. F. Nuttall gave me great help in compiling information in this section.

LIST OF POLITICAL INDEPENDENTS

ALDWORTH, RICHARD. 1647. Bristol.
Rumper.
Son of Robert, mayor of Bristol, well-known merchant family. Mayor himself 1642–3.

ALLANSON, SIR WILLIAM. 1640. York.
Refused to be King's judge, Rumper.
Second son of Christopher, yeoman of Ampleforth. Wool-draper of York. Sheriff 1623–4, mayor 1633–4. Knighted by Charles I. On 102 parliamentary committees up to 1649. Royalist lands (manor and castle of Craike, Yorks.).

ALLEN, FRANCIS. 1645. Cockermouth.
Fled to Army 1647, refused to sign death warrant, Rumper.
Parentage unknown. Goldsmith of St Dunstan's-in-the-West, Fleet Street. Commissioner of Customs 1643, alderman 1647. Bishops' and Royalist land.

except for their religious affiliations, rather redundant. She has not dealt with the Recruiter M.P.'s however, so, for the sake of completeness, I have still included the notes on the original members in my list and added any important sociological considerations noted in her book.

Appendix A

Presbyterian elder of St Dunstan's-in-the-West, although the minister, William Strong, was Independent,[1] and Baillie suggests that he became an Independent.[2]

ALURED, JOHN. 1640. Hedon.
Regicide, Rumper, Colonel.
Son and heir of Henry, Sutton-on-Derwent. Charterhouse, Hull. No parliamentary activity after 1649. Income of £400–£500 p.a. in 1638.[3]
Parish minister the Independent, Josiah Holdsworth.[4]

ANDREWS, ROBERT. 1646. Weobley.
Purged, Rumper.
Parentage unknown. London merchant. Lord Mayor 1650, nominee of Independents. Bishops' land.
Religion possibly Independent.[5]

ANLABY, JOHN. 1647. Scarborough.
Refused to be King's judge, Rumper, Saints' Parliament, both Protectorate Parliaments.
Son and heir of Thomas, Etton, Yorks. Gray's Inn. J.P. m.d. of Sir William Boynton. Little activity before 1649.[6] Pro-Quaker.[7]

ARMINE, SIR WILLIAM. 1641. Grantham (see *D.N.B.*).
Fled to Army, possibly purged, refused to be King's judge, Rumper.
Son and heir of Sir William, Osgodby, Lincs. Sidney Sussex, Cambridge. Sheriff. m.d. of Earl of Shrewsbury. Wealthy and a man of note in his county.[8]
Lady Armine a noted nonconformist, while he wrote as 'one of the Saints' to Cromwell.[9]

ARMINE, SIR WM., JR. 1646. Cumberland.
Possibly purged, entered dissent Feb. 1649, war service.
Son and heir of Sir William (above). Gray's Inn.

[1] W. A. Shaw, *History of the English Church during the Civil Wars*, II, 403, and Ira Brosely, *Ministers of the Abbey Independent Church* (see references to William Strong).
[2] Baillie, *Letters and Journals*, II, 353.
[3] Mary F. Keeler, *The Long Parliament, 1640–1641.*
[4] A. G. Matthews, *Calamy Revised.*
[5] *Congregational Hist. Soc. Trans.* XIII, 151ff.
[6] *Yorks. Arch. Soc. Records*, series 96, p. 51.
[7] Braithwaite, *Beginnings of Quakerism*, p. 119 n. 3.
[8] M. F. Keeler, *op. cit.*
[9] *C.R.* pp. 300, 455, 467; *D.N.B.*, and *Original Letters and Papers of State Addressed to Oliver Cromwell*, ed. J. Nickolls, p. 19.

ARTHINGTON, HENRY. 1646. Pontefract.

Purged, refused to be King's judge, Rumper, excluded from Second Protectorate Parliament.

Son and heir of William of Arthington, Yorks. m.d. of Lord Ferdinando Fairfax.[1] Little activity in Parliament.

ASHE, EDWARD. 1640. Heytesbury.

Rumper.

Younger brother of John (below). Citizen and draper of London, with estates at Heytesbury, Wiltshire. Bishops' land.[2]

ASHE, JAMES. 1645. Bath.

Rumper, both Protectorate Parliaments.

Son and heir of John (below), Freshford, Somerset. Inner Temple Recorder of Bath.

ASHE, JOHN. 1640. Westbury.

Purged, readmitted 3 Feb. 1649, refused to be King's judge, Rumper, both Protectorate Parliaments.

Son and heir of James of Westcombe in Batscombe, Somerset. Described in 1637 as the 'greatest clothier in England'. Attacked monopolies and ecclesiastical abuses.[3] Led Parliamentary Army in Somerset. Advanced £1200 to Parliament. Chairman of Goldsmiths Hall Commission. Presbyterian elder.[4] Gave evidence against Laud.[5]

ATKINS, THOMAS. 1640. Norwich.

Rumper, refused to be King's judge.

Son and heir of John, mayor of King's Lynn. Sheriff and mayor of Norwich. Moved to London, where sheriff 1637, alderman 1638, mayor 1644–5. Imprisoned over forced loan. Leading London Independent,[6] on eighty-eight parliamentary committees, no activity after 1653.

BACON, NATHANIEL. 1645. Cambridge University (see *D.N.B.*).

Purged, readmitted to Parliament 1 June, 1649,[7] Rumper, little activity, both Protectorate Parliaments.

---

[1] C. R. Markham, *Fairfax*, 346.

[2] Brunton and Pennington, *Members of the Long Parliament*, p. 59.

[3] S. W. B. Harbin, *Somerset Arch. Nat. Hist. Soc. Trans.* (1939); see Appendix on M.P.'s.

[4] Shaw, *op. cit.* II, 415.   [5] Harbin, *loc. cit.*

[6] Brunton and Pennington, *op. cit.* pp. 60–61, and C. Walker, *History of Independency*, II, 183.

[7] Brunton and Pennington, *op. cit.* pp. 104–5.

Third son of Edward of Shrubland Hall, Suffolk. Lawyer and writer of Crowfield, Suffolk. Recorder of Ipswich. Big financial gains. Strongly pro-Parliament, very active on Cambridge Committee 1645.

Presbyterian elder[1] but in 1659 appointed trustee for the Independent University of Harvard, New England.[2]

BAINTON, SIR EDWARD. 1640. Chippenham.
Refused to be King's judge, Rumper, both Protectorate Parliaments.
Son and heir of Sir Henry and Lucy Danvers of Broham, Wilts. Knighted 1613. Sheriff of Wilts. 1637. Sometimes voted with Presbyterians.[3] Christ Church, Oxford. Income of £1800–£2000 p.a. in 1657.[4] Friend of Henry Marten.
Held advowson of Broham Church, where W. Hughes, Independent, was made curate 1639.[5]

BAKER, JOHN. 1645. East Grinstead.
Rumper.
Son and heir of Michael, Mayfield, Sussex. Magdalen, Oxford and Inner Temple.

BAMFIELD, JOHN. 1640. Penryn (d. 1650).
Fled to Army.
Son and heir of John, Poltimore, Devon. Oxford and Middle Temple. Very rich. His son had £1900 p.a. in 1660.[6]
Son was an Independent minister.[7]

BARKSTEAD, JOHN. 1654. Middlesex (see *D.N.B.*).
Regicide, both Protectorate Parliaments, Colonel.
Silversmith, then goldsmith, the Strand, London. Bishops' land. Independent. Commended the Congregational way at his execution.[8]

BARRINGTON, SIR JOHN. 1646. Newtown, Isle of Wight.
Absent at Pride's Purge.[9] Refused to be King's judge and withdrew from politics after King's death.[10]

---

[1] Shaw, *op. cit.* II, 426.
[2] W. L. Sachse, 'Migration of New Englanders to England', *American Hist. Rev.* LIII, 276.
[3] *Commons Journals*, e.g. 19 March 1648.
[4] M. F. Keeler, *op. cit.*   [5] *C.R.*
[6] M. F. Keeler, *op. cit.*   [7] *C.R.*
[8] Howell, *State Trials*, V, 1325.
[9] *Essex Arch. Soc. Trans.* II, 22, 38, and (1945), p. 282.
[10] *Ibid.*

Son and heir of Sir Thomas, Barrington Hall, Essex, who was imprisoned over forced loan 1623 and took part in colonizing activity. Trinity, Cambridge and Gray's Inn. Cousin of Cromwell and friend of Pym.[1] Estates near Hatfield, Herts. Indebted £10,000.
Presbyterian.[2] Installed J. Warren, Independent, as parish minister.[3]

BENNETT, ROBERT. 1648. West Looe.
Rumper, Saints' Parliament, First Protectorate Parliament, war service.
Son and heir of Richard, Lawhilton, Hexworthy, Cornwall. Exeter College, Oxford and Middle Temple. Alderman of Launceston. Friend of Cromwell. Republican. Royalist land.[4]
Baptist.[5]

BETHEL, SLINGSBY. 1659. Knaresborough (see *D.N.B.*).
Richard Cromwell's Parliament.
Third son of Sir Walter, Alne. London merchant. Bought some estates of his Royalist uncle. 'Shimei' of *Absalom and Achitophel*. 'A known republican in principle...a sullen and wilful man...had expressed his approving of the late king's death in very indecent terms.' Wrote *The World's Mistake in Oliver Cromwell*.
Independent.

BINGHAM, JOHN. 1645. Shaftesbury.
Fled to Army, Rumper, Saints' Parliament, both Protectorate Parliaments, war service.
Son and heir of Richard, Bingham Melcombe, Dorset. Very old family.[6] Brasenose, Oxford and Middle Temple.
House licensed for Independent worship 1672.[7]

BIRCH, THOMAS. 1649. Liverpool.
Rumper, First Protectorate Parliament, excluded from Second Protectorate Parliament, war service.
Son and heir of George, Birch Hall, nr. Manchester. Cousin of John Birch, Presbyterian member of Parliament for Leominster.
Independent.[8]

---

[1] Brunton and Pennington, *op. cit.* pp. 123–4.
[2] Shaw, *op. cit.* II, 382.   [3] *C.R.*
[4] M. Coate, *Cornwall in the Great Civil War*, pp. 252, 272.
[5] George Fox, *Journals* (ed. Penney), I, 228.
[6] A. R. Bayley, *Civil War in Dorset*, p. 30.
[7] G. Lyon-Turner, *Original Records of Early Nonconformity*, p. 1139.
[8] R. Halley, *Lancashire, its Puritanism and Nonconformity*, p. 161.

Appendix A

BLACKSTON, JOHN. 1641. Newcastle (see *D.N.B.*).
Fled to Army, Regicide, Rumper.
Son of Archdeacon of York. Mercer of Newcastle. Subscribed £450 or £750 to Irish war 1642 but probably not wealthy.[1] Church lands. Influenced by Haselrig.
Very religious Puritan.[2] Before Court of High Commission.

BLAGRAVE, DANIEL. 1645. Reading (see *D.N.B.*).
Regicide, Rumper, Second Protectorate Parliament.
Third son of Anthony of Southcott, Berks. Middle Temple?[3] Lawyer and Recorder of Reading. Church and Royalist land.
Puritan. Severe against Anglican ministers.

BLAKE, ROBERT. 1645. Bridgwater (see *D.N.B.*).
Rumper, war service, Saints' Parliament, both Protectorate Parliaments.
Son and heir of Humphrey, Planchfield, Somerset, whose estate was £200 p.a. Wadham, Oxford. Successful merchant of Bridgwater.[4] Early Republican. Admiral.
Presbyterian elder.[5] Devout Puritan.[6]

BOND, DENIS. 1640. Dorchester (see *D.N.B.*).
Refused to be King's judge, Rumper, both Protectorate Parliaments.
Son and heir of John of Lutton, Isle of Purbeck. Estate at Lutton. Woollen draper, probably not wealthy.[7] Friend of Cromwell. No suspicion of peculation. On 263 parliamentary committees. 'Very severe and resolved against the Church and Court.'[8]
Disciple of White, the radical Puritan founder of Dorchester Colonizing Company.

BOONE, THOMAS. 1646. Clifton–Dartmouth.
Fled to Army, refused to be King's judge, Rumper, first Protectorate Parliament.
Origins uncertain, but a man of influence. Merchant trading with Spain. On sixty-three parliamentary committees. Cromwell's Ambassador to Russia.[9]
Independent? Friend of James Birdwood, radical Puritan.[10]

---

[1] M. F. Keeler, *op. cit.*
[2] A. Barnes, *Memoirs* (Surtees Soc. 1886), pp. 322, 327.
[3] Brunton and Pennington, *op. cit.* p. 34.
[4] Harbin, *op. cit.*   [5] Shaw, *op. cit.* II, 421.
[6] M. P. Ashley, *Cromwell's Generals*, p. 119.
[7] M. F. Keeler, *op. cit.*   [8] Clarendon, *op. cit.* II, § 27.
[9] *Devonshire Assoc. Trans.* XLIII, 173, 353.
[10] C.R. See also *Congregational Hist. Soc. Trans.* XIII, 'The Dartmouth Congregational Church'.

BOSVILLE, GODFREY. 1640. Warwick.
Fled to Army (Percival), refused to be King's judge, Rumper, war service.
Son and heir of Sir Robert, Wroxhall, Warwick, and Gunthwaite, Yorks. Yorks properties of 800 acres.[1] Brother-in-law of Haselrig.
Connected by marriage with a leader of Massachusetts Bay Company[2] though son tutored by Joseph Shaw, who was a Presbyterian.[3]

BOURCHIER, SIR JOHN. 1647. Ripon (see *D.N.B.*).
Regicide, Rumper.
Son and heir of William, Benningborough, Yorks, and grandson of Lord Montague. With estates.[4] Christ's, Cambridge, and Gray's Inn. Clashed with Strafford over enclosure, and with Charles over alum mines.[5] Friend of Lord Warwick.[6] Virginia Company. 'A rigid Independent and Republican.'
Wrote to Fairfax on want of good ministers in Yorks.

BRADSHAW, JOHN. 1654. Stafford (see *D.N.B.*).
Regicide, President of the Court trying the King, first Protectorate Parliament.
Third son of an 'ancient family...but a fortune of his own making'.[7] Gray's Inn. Lawyer. Mayor of Congleton 1637. Moved to London 1643. Chief Justice of Chester 1646-7. Much legal business for the Rump. Royalist lands.
Probably Independent, certainly Puritan. Friendly to Quakers.[8]

BRERETON, SIR WILLIAM. 1640. Cheshire (see *D.N.B.*).
Fled to Army (Percival), purged, refused to be King's judge, Rumper, second Protectorate Parliament, war service.
Son and heir of William, Handforth, Cheshire. Brasenose, Oxford, and Gray's Inn. Massachusetts Bay Company.[9] Royalist and bishops' lands. 'Notable courage and sobriety' and 'competent fortune'.[10]
Presbyterian elder[11] yet had Independent chaplain.[12] Strong Puritan[13] impressed by Hugh Peters.[14]

---

[1] M. F. Keeler, *op. cit.*   [2] *Ibid.*
[3] R. W. Dale, *History of Congregationalism in Yorkshire*, p. 143.
[4] *Victoria County History of Yorkshire*, II, 162.
[5] *Ibid.* III, 282.
[6] A. P. Newton, *Colonising Activity of the English Puritans*, p. 78.
[7] Clarendon, *op. cit.* XI, § 220.   [8] Fox, *op. cit.* I, 409.
[9] Brunton and Pennington, *op. cit.* p. 66.
[10] Clarendon, *op. cit.* VI, § 272.   [11] Shaw, *op. cit.* II, 435.
[12] C.R. under George Moxon.   [13] Clarendon, *op. cit.* VI, § 269.
[14] William Brereton, *Travels in Holland* (Chetham Soc. Vol. I), p. 6.

Appendix A

BREWSTER, ROBERT. 1645. Dunwich.

Rumper, both Protectorate Parliaments, war service.

Son and heir of Francis, Wrentham Hall, Suffolk. Gentry of consideration in their county for a long time. Pembroke, Cambridge. Wrentham Manor worth £700 p.a. m.d. of Sir John Corbet of Sprowston, Norfolk. Bought lands of Bishop of Norwich worth £300 p.a.[1] Pro-Cromwell and kingship party.

Presbyterian elder[2] yet in fact an Independent.[3] Strong Puritan family.

BROOKE, PETER. 1646. Newton-in-Mattersfield.

Purged, Rumper, second Protectorate Parliament.

Third son but heir (Pink) of Thomas of Norton Priory, Cheshire. Bought Mere Manor 1652. In Booth's conspiracy of 1659 to bring in Chas. II. Knighted 1660.[4]

Presbyterian elder.[5]

BROWNE, JOHN. 1640. Dorset.

Rumper, refused to sign death warrant, war service.

Son and heir of Sir John of Frampton, Dorset. Magdalen, Oxford and Middle Temple. Monastic lands.[6] Sheriff of Dorset 1632–3. In Dorchester Colonizing Company. Family of wealth and influence. His father left him £1000 p.a. and he added much more. m.d. of Sir George Trenchard. Clashed with Laud. In trouble with Charles' government for civil and religious reasons. On ninety-six parliamentary committees.

Strong Puritan and friend of John White of Dorchester.[7]

BURRELL, ABRAHAM. 1645. Huntingdon.

Rumper, refused to be King's judge.

Second son of Richard. Merchant of London, in Grocers' Company. Brother of Sir John the Royalist. Estates in Hampshire.[8]

CAREW, JOHN. Tregony (see *D.N.B.*).

Regicide, Rumper, Saints' Parliament, second Protectorate Parliament.

Third son of Richard of Antony. Gloucester Hall, Oxford and Inner Temple. Large estates and church land.[9] Republican.

Baptist and Fifth Monarchist.[10]

---

[1] W. A. Copinger, *The Manors of Suffolk*, II, 212; Brunton and Pennington, *op. cit.* p. 110.　　[2] Shaw, *op. cit.* II, 435.

[3] J. Browne, *History of Congregationalism in Norfolk and Suffolk*, pp. 421 ff.

[4] *Life of Adam Martindale* (Chetham Soc. vol. IV), p. 141.

[5] Shaw, *op. cit.* p. 395.　　[6] Brunton and Pennington, *op. cit.* p. 161.

[7] M. F. Keeler, *op. cit.*

[8] *Victoria County History of Huntingdonshire*, II, 28, 319.

[9] M. Coate, *op. cit.* p. 247.　　[10] *Ibid.* p. 286.

CAWLEY, WILLIAM. 1640. Midhurst (see *D.N.B.*).
Regicide, Rumper.
Son and heir of John, brewer and mayor of Chichester. One of richest
and most influential men in West Sussex, worth £2100 in 1663. Fined
for distraint of knighthood 1628.[1] Hart Hall, Oxford and Gray's Inn.
Puritan. Held living of Rotherfield and installed his son.[2]

CECIL, WILLIAM, 2nd Earl of Salisbury. 1649. King's Lynn.
Rumper, first Protectorate Parliament, excluded from second.
St John's, Cambridge and Gray's Inn. One of the few Parliamentary
peers and therefore greatly used by Parliament. Bishops' land.
Member of Westminster Assembly.[3]

CHALLONER, JAMES. 1643. Aldborough (see *D.N.B.*).
Refused to sign King's death warrant, Rumper.
Fourth son of Sir Thomas of Yorkshire, who had been tutor to Henry
Prince of Wales, and friend of Cecil, and whose alum mines were seized
by Charles. m.d. of Sir William Fairfax. Active in Parliament.

CHALLONER, THOMAS. 1645. Richmond (see *D.N.B.*).
Regicide, Rumper.
Third son of Sir Thomas of Yorkshire. Brasenose, Oxford and Middle
Temple. Held manor of Steeple Claydon, Bucks, in trust for nephew,
and after 1647 Rectory Manor as composition for brother Henry.[4]
Estates in Yorks. Strong Republican. Bishops' land.
Theist. 'One of Henry Marten's Gang' (Noble).

CLEMENT, GREGORY. 1647. Fowey (see *D.N.B.*).
Regicide, Rumper.
Merchant of Plymouth and London, trading with Spain. Big gains from
war. Expelled from Parliament for immorality.

CONSTABLE, SIR WILLIAM. 1642. Knaresborough (see *D.N.B.*).
Fled to Army, Regicide, Rumper, war service.
Son and heir of Sir Robert of Flamborough, who was involved in Essex
plot. 'Ancient but decayed family.' In debt 1630–40. m.d. of 1st Lord
Fairfax. Bishops' land.
William Sedgewick, Fifth Monarchist and mystic, was his army chaplain.
Commended by the churches of Gloucestershire for his 'tenderness to
God's people'.[5] Baxter calls him an Independent.[6]

---

[1] C. W. Thomas-Stanford, *Sussex in the Great Civil War*, p. 319.
[2] *Ibid.* p. 302. [3] Brunton and Pennington, *op. cit.* p. 106.
[4] *Victoria County History of Buckinghamshire*, IV, 227, and Bucks Hist. Soc.
Records, V, 78.
[5] *Original Letters and Papers of State Addressed to Oliver Cromwell*, ed.
J. Nickolls, p. 125. [6] Richard Baxter, 'Penitent Confession' (1690).

Appendix A

COOK, JOHN (see *D.N.B.*).
Regicide.
Gray's Inn. Lawyer. Leading Republican. Spent most of his time in Ireland. Supported Lilburne 1646.
Independent. Wrote 'What the Independents Would Have'.

CORBET, JOHN. 1645. Bishop's Castle.
Fled to Army, refused to be King's judge, Rumper.
Son and heir of Richard of Halston, Shropshire. Gray's Inn. Church lands. Chief Justice in Protectorate.
Presbyterian elder.[1]

CORBET, MILES. 1640. Great Yarmouth (see *D.N.B.*).
Fled to Army, Regicide, Rumper.
Second son of Sir Thomas of Sprowston, Norfolk. Christ's, Cambridge, and Lincoln's Inn. Lawyer. Recorder of Yarmouth and King's Lynn. Baron of Exchequer in Ireland 1655. A man of integrity.[2]
Member of Yarmouth Independent Church.[3]

CROMWELL, OLIVER. 1640. Cambridge (see *D.N.B.*).
Fled to Army (Percival), Regicide, Rumper, Lord Protector.
Son and heir of Robert, Huntingdon. Sidney Sussex, Cambridge, and Lincoln's Inn. Family estates gained at Dissolution of Monasteries were wasted by extravagance in time of James I. He 'belonged in substance to the lesser gentry though his family antecedents were much more distinguished'.[4]
An Independent of a radical variety, though supported classical Independents when in power.[5]

DANVERS, HENRY.
Saints' Parliament.
Heir to Baynton and West Cowlston. Christ Church, Oxford and Gray's Inn. Governor of Stafford 1651.
Baptist.[6]

DANVERS, SIR JOHN. 1645. Malmesbury (see *D.N.B.*).
Fled to Army, Regicide, Rumper.
Younger brother and heir of Earl of Danby. Brasenose, Oxford. 'Neglected by his brother...by a vain expense in his way of living contracted a vast debt.'[7] Bishops' land.

[1] Shaw, *op. cit.* II, 407.   [2] Brunton and Pennington, *op. cit.* p. 80.
[3] J. Browne, *op. cit.* p. 230.   [4] Brunton and Pennington, *op. cit.* p. 113.
[5] *Writings and Speeches* (ed. Abbott), III, 436. Speech to first Protectorate Parliament.
[6] A. G. Matthews, *The Congregational Churches of Staffordshire*, p. 34.
[7] Clarendon, *op. cit.* XI, § 237.

DARLEY, HENRY. 1641. Northallerton.

Fled to Army, absent during Pride's Purge,[1] Rumper, excluded from second Protectorate Parliament.

Son and heir of Sir Richard of Buttercrombe, Yorks. Trinity, Cambridge and Gray's Inn. Friend of Winthrop and Pym. Imprisoned 1640. Massachusetts Bay, Saybrook and Connecticut Colonizing Companies.[2] Very active in Parliament before and after Pride's Purge. On committee to Scotland with Vane and Armine 1643. m.d. of William Watts, lawyer of London. Bishops' lands. Strong Republican.

Planned to migrate to New England under Laudian persecution.[3] With his brother, helped Thomas Shephard, Puritan minister ejected by Laud.[4]

DARLEY, RICHARD. 1645. New Malton.

Refused to be King's judge, Rumper, excluded from second Protectorate Parliament.

Third son of Sir Richard of Buttercrombe, Yorks. Very active in Parliament. m.d. of Sir William Hildyard of Bishop Burton.[5]

See above, Henry Darley.

DEANE, RICHARD (see *D.N.B.*).

Regicide, war service.

Younger son of Edward of Temple Guiting, Gloucester. Mercantile career in London with help of uncle Sir Richard (mayor and shipowner, well-known Puritan, whose daughters married Mildmay and Goodwin). Radical associates.

Fifth Monarchist.[6]

DESBOROUGH, JOHN (see *D.N.B.*).

Refused to be King's judge, both Protectorate Parliaments, war service.

Second son of Sir James of Eltisley, Cambridge. Law and small-holding (£60–£70 p.a.). m. Cromwell's sister.

Independent. 1672 on a list of John Owen's congregation.[7] Younger brother went to Connecticut 1639.

DIXWELL, JOHN. 1646. Dover (see *D.N.B.*).

Regicide, Rumper, both Protectorate Parliaments, war service.

Younger son of William of Broome, Kent. Younger yet wealthy branch of Warwickshire family settled in Kent *temp*. James I.[8]

Met with Oxinden and Boys in a gathered Church under John Barton.[9]

[1] Whitelocke, *Memorials*, III, 32.   [2] A. P. Newton, *op. cit.* p. 125.
[3] *Ibid.* p. 245.
[4] *Yorks. Arch. Soc. Records* (1938), p. 74.
[5] *Ibid.* p. 78.
[6] L. Brown, *Political Activities of Baptists and Fifth Monarchy Men*, p. 10.
[7] *Congregational Hist. Soc. Trans.* I, 27.
[8] Hastead, *Kent*, VIII, 93, 160; IX, 354–5.   [9] E. Calamy, *Account*, p. 536.

Appendix A

DORMER, JOHN. 1646. Buckingham.
Rumper.
Son and heir of Sir Fleetwood, Shipton Lee, Quainton, Bucks. Magdalen, Oxford and Lincoln's Inn. Practising barrister.

DOVE, JOHN. 1645. Salisbury (see *D.N.B.*).
Survived Purge?[1] King's judge but refused to sign death warrant. Rumper.
Alderman of Salisbury. Royalist and church lands. Careerist.

DOWNES, JOHN. 1641. Arundel (see *D.N.B.*).
Regicide, Rumper, war service.
Said to be of a poor London family, but probably barrister of Inner Temple. Bought auditorship of Duchy of Cornwall 1635. Much church and royalist land.[2]

DRYDEN, SIR JOHN. 1640. Northamptonshire.
Rumper.
Son and heir of Sir Erasmus, a strong Puritan. A man of considerable wealth. Resisted ship money and was threatened with Star Chamber proceedings. Broodgates Hall, Oxford and Middle Temple.
Clashed with Laud over absence of conformist ministers in his parish.[3]

DUNCH, EDMUND. 1640. Wallingford.
Fled to Army, Rumper, both Protectorate Parliaments, war service.
Son and heir of Sir William of Little Wittenham, Berks. Former monastic lands. Very wealthy—owned at least twelve manors. Co-heir to Burnell Barony.[4] Sheriff of Berks. 1633-4. Gray's Inn.
Independent congregation met in his house 1669.[5]

EDWARDS, HUMPHREY. 1646. Shropshire (see *D.N.B.*).
Fled to Army, Regicide, Rumper.
Second son of Thomas, sheriff of Shropshire. His Royalist brother inherited most of estate. He had £100 p.a. from his share, and legacy of £500 p.a. and land at Moel Brace. Gray's Inn. At first Royalist, but sided with Parliament 1642. Fraudulent election.[6]

EDWARDS, RICHARD. 1646. Christchurch.
Rumper, first Protectorate Parliament.
Lawyer, m.d. of Sir Henry Whitehead, Norman Court, Hants.[7]

[1] See Appendix B, n. 2.
[2] *Sussex Arch. Soc. Trans.* LII, 21; M. F. Keeler, *op. cit.*
[3] M. F. Keeler, *op. cit.*
[4] *Victoria County History of Berkshire*, IV, 382; M. F. Keeler, *op. cit.*
[5] *C.R.* under John Wells.
[6] *Shropshire Arch. and Nat. Hist. Soc. Trans.* (1880), p. 141; (1927-8), pp. 173-5.   [7] Brunton and Pennington, *op. cit.* p. 31.

ELLIS, WILLIAM. 1640. Boston (see *D.N.B.*).

Purged, Rumper, both Protectorate Parliaments.

Second son of Sir Thomas of Grantham. Royalist family. Considerable estate. Christ's, Cambridge, and Gray's Inn. Solicitor-General 1654.

Matthew Bloom, Presbyterian-Congregationalist, died at his house.[1] Presbyterian elder.[2]

ERLE, ERASMUS. 1647. Norwich.

Rumper.

Son of Thomas of Salle, Norfolk. Peterhouse, Cambridge, and Lincoln's Inn. Prominent lawyer of Norwich. Active locally but often absent from Parliament.

Very moderate to Quakers.[3]

EVELYN, SIR JOHN. 1640. Ludgershall.

Fled to Army, purged.

Son and heir of George of West Dean and Everley, Wilts. Also held Pitton Grange. Lands worth £2000 p.a. though in debt for £7000. Emmanuel, Cambridge. Exempted from royal pardon 1642 and consistently radical until 1648. m.d. of Robert Cockes, and their d. married Duke of Kingston. Church lands.[4]

D'Ewes says he became an opponent of the Presbyterian church system August 1643.[5]

EYE, WILLIAM. 1648. Chippenham.

Rumper, second Protectorate Parliament, war service.

Son and heir of Sir William of Neston, Wilts. Pembroke, Cambridge.

EWERS, ISAAC (see *D.N.B.*).

Regicide, war service.

Origins obscure. Great gains by war.

FAGGE, JOHN. 1645. Rye (see *D.N.B.*).

King's judge, but did not sign death warrant, Rumper, first Protectorate Parliament, excluded from second, war service.

Son and heir of John, Nye and Wiston, Sussex. Estates. m.d. of Robert Morley and completely under his influence.[6] Offered Parliament £1000 in 1643. Baronet at Restoration.[7]

Helped ejected clergy.[8]

[1] *C.R.*

[2] Shaw, *op. cit.* II, 404. This could be a case of misidentification.

[3] Swathmore MSS. pp. 4, 156.

[4] M. F. Keeler, *op. cit.* and Hoare, *History of Wiltshire*, V, 23, 41 for material on Evelyn.   [5] D'Ewes MSS. (B.M. Harleian 165), folios 157ff.

[6] Thomas-Stanford, *op. cit.* p. 288.   [7] *Ibid.* p. 315.

[8] *C.R.* under John Beaton.

FAIRFAX, SIR THOMAS. 1644. Cirencester (see *D.N.B.*).

Refused to be King's judge, General, elected to first Protectorate Parliament.

Third Baron Fairfax, son of Lord Ferdinando, Denton, Yorks. St John's, Cambridge and Gray's Inn. Withdrew from politics after 1649. Bishops' land.

Richard Stretton, Presbyterian, and Edmund Dell, mystic, were his chaplains.[1] Wife a Presbyterian.[2] Daughter Independent.[3]

FELL, THOMAS. 1645. Lancaster (see *D.N.B.*).

Rumper.

Son and heir of George of Swathmore Hall, Ulverston, Lancs. University College, Oxford and Gray's Inn. Judge. Anti-Cromwellian.

Presbyterian elder.[4] Allowed Quaker meetings in his home. Widow later married George Fox.

FENWICK, GEORGE. 1645. Morpeth (see *D.N.B.*).

Fled to Army, refused to be King's judge, Rumper, first Protectorate Parliament, excluded from second, war service.

Son and heir of George, Brinkburn, Northumberland. Queens', Cambridge and Gray's Inn. m.d. of Haselrig. In New England 1635–40. At one time a merchant of Newcastle. Bishops' land.

Defended Blackston in Court of High Commission.[5] The Independent, R. Ward, was chaplain of his regiment.[6]

FIELDER, JOHN. 1647. St Ives.

Rumper, war service.

Son and heir of John, Borough Court and Odiham, Hants. Did not appear in House until 1649. Took no part in Protectorate.

FIENNES, JOHN. 1645. Morpeth (see *D.N.B.*).

Fled to Army, purged, war service.

Third son of Lord Say and Sele. Bishops' land. m.d. of Thomas Hobbes. 'Such a one as they call a sectary, but no great stickler.'

FIENNES, NATHANIEL. 1640. Banbury (see *D.N.B.*).

Fled to Army, purged, both Protectorate Parliaments, war service.

Second son of Lord Say and Sele. New College, Oxford. Sided with Independents until Nov. 1648 and later supported Cromwell.

Strong Puritan. Appointed John Tombes, Baptist, vicar of All Saints, Bristol, 1643.

---

[1] *C.R.*   [2] R. W. Dale, *History of Congregationalism in Yorkshire.*
[3] *Congregational Hist. Soc. Trans.* IX, 31.
[4] Shaw, *op. cit.* II, 390.
[5] *Records of the High Commission Court in the Diocese of Durham* (Surtees Soc. vol. XXXIV), p. 162.
[6] *C.R.*

FIENNES, LORD WILLIAM. Say and Sele (see *D.N.B.*).
Son and heir of Lord Say and Sele. Imprisoned 1622 over benevolence. Colonizing promoter with Pym and Lord Brooke. A centre of Puritan opposition to Charles.[1] The only real Independent in House of Lords.[2] Sided with Army until Aug. 1647, then worked for peace.
Regarded as a leading Independent by Baillie[3] but no Separatist.

FLEETWOOD, CHARLES. 1645. Marlborough (see *D.N.B.*).
Refused to be King's judge, Rumper, both Protectorate Parliaments, war service.
Son and heir of Sir Miles of Wood St., London and Aldwinkle, Northants. Emmanuel, Cambridge, and Gray's Inn. m. Cromwell's daughter.
Independent. John Owen's congregation.[4]

FLEETWOOD, GEORGE. 1645. Buckinghamshire (see *D.N.B.*).
Regicide, Rumper, Saints' Parliament, first Protectorate Parliament, war service.
Son and heir of Charles, Chalfont St Giles, Bucks.
Sectary.

FOULKES, JOHN. 1661. London (see *D.N.B.*).
Refused to be King's judge.
Third son of William of Tewkesbury. Haberdashers' Company, London. Very rich. Refused tonnage and poundage. Exempted from pardon 1641. Alderman 1642. Bishops' land.
Pro-Independent 1647.[5] Anabaptist.[6]

FRY, JOHN. 1647. Shaftesbury (see *D.N.B.*).
Survived Purge, King's judge but refused to sign death warrant, excluded from Rump 1651.
Son and heir of William of Twene Minster, Dorset. Very active in Parliament.
Religion unorthodox. Unitarian?

GARLAND, AUGUSTINE. 1648. Queensborough (see *D.N.B.*).
Regicide, Rumper, first Protectorate Parliament.
Son and heir of Augustine, Tulsham Hall, Kent. Emmanuel, Cambridge and Lincoln's Inn. An attorney of Coleman Street, London.

---

[1] Clarendon, *op. cit.* III, § 26.   [2] *Ibid.* VIII, § 260.

[3] Baillie, *Letters and Journals*, II, 146, 240, 344.

[4] *Congregational Hist. Soc. Trans.* I, 27.

[5] Holles, *Memoirs*, in Maseres, *Tracts*, I, 254, 282; Walker, *op. cit.* II, 85, who refers to him as 'one of the godly'.

[6] Pepys, *Diary* (ed. H. B. Wheatley), I, 362.

GIBBS, WILLIAM. 1654. Suffolk.
First Protectorate Parliament, excluded from second.
Son of Henry of Comerton, Snoke Hazeland, Suffolk. Goldsmiths' Company, London. Alderman 1642.
Pro-Independent 1647.[1] Spoke for a godly ministry.[2]

GOFFE, WILLIAM. 1654. Great Yarmouth (see *D.N.B.*).
Regicide, both Protectorate Parliaments, war service.
Son of Stephen, rector of Stanmore, Sussex. Apprenticed in London. m.d. of Whalley.
Independent[3] and Fifth Monarchist.[4]

GOLD, NICHOLAS. April 1648. Fowey.
Rumper.
Fifth son of Edward of Staverton. Plymouth merchant.[5]

GOODWIN, JOHN. 1640. Haslemere.
Refused to be King's judge, Rumper, first Protectorate Parliament, excluded from second.
Second son of Edward, Horne, Surrey. Inner Temple.
m.d. of R. Deane, mayor of London. Church and royalist lands.[6]
Presbyterian elder.[7]

GOODWIN, ROBERT. 1640. East Grinstead.
Fled to Army (Percival), active Rumper.
Son and heir of Edward of Horne, Surrey. A man of moderate wealth with at least five manors.[8] Church and royalist lands.
Presbyterian elder.[9]

GRATEWICKE, ROGER.
Refused to be King's judge, Rumper.
Third son of Sir William, Seaford, Sussex.

GREY, LORD, OF GROBY. 1640. Leicester (see *D.N.B.*).
Fled to Army, active part in Pride's Purge, Regicide, Rumper, first Protectorate Parliament, war service.

---

[1] Holles, *op. cit.*
[2] Burton, *Parliamentary Diary*, II, 334.
[3] *Congregational Hist. Soc. Trans.* I, 27.
[4] See Putney Debates in Woodhouse, *Puritanism and Liberty*, pp. 19–20, 39–42.
[5] M. Coate, *op. cit.* p. 245.
[6] *Victoria County History of Surrey*, II, 604, and III, 235.
[7] Shaw, *op. cit.* II, 434.   [8] M. F. Keeler, *op. cit.*
[9] Shaw, *op. cit.* II, 434.

Son and heir of the Puritan Earl of Stamford and the d. of William Cecil. Gray's Inn. Manors of Bradgate, Stamford, and lands in Charnwood Forest. Great wealth and influence.[1] Great gains in war, e.g. Craven estates worth £3000 p.a. Very active and radical throughout. Fifth Monarchist?[2]

GURDON, BRAMPTON, JR. 1645. Sudbury.
Purged, Rumper.
Third son of Brampton of Assington, Suffolk. Owned Letton, Suffolk. Bishops' land.
Presbyterian elder[3] yet his tutor had been the Baptist, Henry Jessey.[4]

GURDON, JOHN. 1640. Ipswich (see *D.N.B.*).
Refused to be King's judge, Rumper, first Protectorate Parliament.
Son and heir of Brampton. Income £1400 p.a. in 1655.[5] Emmanuel, Cambridge and Gray's Inn. Little activity during Protectorate.
Presbyterian elder[6] but friend of Winthrop of Massachusetts.[7] Minister of Assington was radical.[8]

HALLOWES, NATHANIEL. 1640. Derby.
Fled to Army (Percival), Rumper.
Son of Samuel. Owned Dronfield, Derby, but not wealthy.[9] Alderman and mayor of Derby 1657. Bishops' land.
Father an Independent.[10]

HARBY, EDWARD. 1645. Higham Ferrers.
Rumper, but not active.
Son and heir of Francis, Adston, Northants. Lincoln's Inn. Sheriff of Northants. 1643.
Helped ejected nonconformist minister.[11]

HARRINGTON, SIR JAMES. 1645. Rutland (see *D.N.B.*).
King's judge but refused to sign death warrant, Rumper, first Protectorate Parliament.

---

[1] Clarendon, *op. cit.* XIII, §§ 453–4 and Nichols, *Leicestershire*, III, 676ff.
[2] He was arrested in a Fifth Monarchist plot, but I have no other evidence as to his religious inclinations (Nichols, *op. cit.* p. 679).
[3] Shaw, *op. cit.* II, 429.   [4] *C.R.*
[5] M. F. Keeler, *op. cit.*   [6] Shaw, *op. cit.* II, 423.
[7] A. P. Newton, *op. cit.* p. 78.
[8] *C.R.* under T. Walker.   [9] M. F. Keeler, *op. cit.*
[10] *Congregational Hist. Soc. Trans.* VI, 402.
[11] *C.R.* under Robert Allen.

Son and heir of Sir Edward, Kidlington, Rutland. Trinity, Oxford. Knighted 1628. Republican. Active in Parliament. His diary of 1647 would suggest that he did not then regard himself as a political Independent.[1]

Wrote 'Noah's Dove' 1645 urging unity between Presbyterians and Independents in religion.

HARRISON, THOMAS. 1646. Wendover (see *D.N.B.*).
Fled to Army (Percival), Rumper, Regicide, Saints' Parliament, war service.

Son of a butcher and grazier of Newcastle under Lyme. Single-minded religious Republican.

Fifth Monarchist.

HARVEY, EDMUND. 1646. Great Bedwin (see *D.N.B.*).
King's judge but refused to sign death warrant, Rumper, first Protectorate Parliament, excluded from second, war service.

Son and heir of Charles, fishmonger of London. Silk merchant in partnership with Alderman Sleigh.

Much church and royalist land, e.g. Fulham Palace, which 'changed him from a furious Presbyter to a Bedlam Independent'.[2]

HASELRIG, SIR ARTHUR. 1640. Leicestershire (see *D.N.B.*).
Fled to Army, refused to be King's judge, Rumper, first Protectorate Parliament, excluded from second.

Son and heir of Sir Thomas. Great estates in Durham and Leicester. Saybrook Colonizing Company. Friend of Pym. m.d. of Lord Brooke. Personal quarrel with Laud. Much church land. One of 'the five M.P.s', 1641.

Installed an Independent, Samuel Hammond.[3]

HAY, HERBERT. 1645. Arundel.
Purged?[4] Rumper.

Son and heir of John, Glyndebourne, Sussex. Nephew and ward of Herbert Morley and completely under his influence.[5]

HAY, WILLIAM. 1641. Rye.
Rumper, both Protectorate Parliaments.

Brother of above, of Horsted Parva, Sussex. St Catharine's, Cambridge? (Venn). Probably average estates.[6] On twenty-seven Long Parliament committees.

---

[1] British Museum, Additional MSS. 10, 114.
[2] Walker, *op. cit.* II, 13.   [3] *C.R.*
[4] On one exclusion list, but on Committee of Rump, Feb. 1649.
[5] Noble, *Lives of the Regicides.*   [6] M. F. Keeler, *op. cit.*

HERBERT, HENRY. 1642. Monmouthshire.
First Protectorate Parliament, war service.
Son and heir of William of Colebrooke, Monmouth. Magdalen Hall, Oxford. m.d. of James Rudyard of London. Active in Commonwealth. Royalist lands.

HERBERT, LORD PHILIP. 1640. Glamorgan (see *D.N.B.*).
Purged? Rumper. Entered dissent Feb. 1649.
Son and heir of Earl of Pembroke. Lord Lieutenant of Monmouth 1642. Not very active in Parliament. Declining family fortunes repaired by rich marriage 1639.[1]

HEVENINGHAM, WILLIAM. 1640. Stockbridge (see *D.N.B.*).
Rumper, King's judge but refused to sign death warrant.
Son and heir of Sir John of Ketteringham, Suffolk. Pembroke, Cambridge. Sheriff of Norfolk 1633. Bishops' land. m. (i) d. of Sir Henry Wallop, Wilts; (ii) d. of Sir John Carey.
Probably Independent.[2]

HEWSON, JOHN. 1653. Ireland (see *D.N.B.*).
Regicide, Saints' Parliament, first Protectorate Parliament, war service.
'An honest shoe-maker of Westminster.'
Independent[3] and perhaps later Anabaptist.

HEYMAN, HENRY. 1640. Hythe.
Fled to Army,[4] Rumper, entered dissent June 1649.
Son and heir of Sir Peter, Somerfield in Selling, Kent, who refused to pay forced loans. A man of good estate.[5] Active in Parliament.

HILL, ROGER. 1640. Bridport (see *D.N.B.*).
Fled to Army, refused to be King's judge, Rumper.
Son and heir of William, Poundisford, near Taunton. St John's, Cambridge, and Inner Temple. Barrister 1633. 1644 counsel against Laud. Judge under Commonwealth. m. (i) d. of Giles Green, Dorset; (ii) d. of Brampton Gurdon. Much bishops' land, e.g. Taunton Dene.[6] Family connected with Dorchester Colonizing Company.[7]
Presbyterian elder, strongly opposed to episcopacy.[8]

---

[1] M. F. Keeler, *op. cit.*
[2] *C.R.* under N. Leverton and S. Habergham.
[3] Woodhouse, *op. cit.* p. 165. Hewson sided with the Independents against the Separatists.
[4] Rushworth (*Historical Collections*, part IV, p. 755) has 'Hammond'.
[5] M. F. Keeler, *op. cit.* [6] Brunton and Pennington, *op. cit.* p. 171.
[7] F. Rose-Troup, *op. cit.* p. 449.
[8] Shaw, *op. cit.* II, 421, and D'Ewes *Journal*, ed. Notestein, p. 426.

HIPPSLEY, SIR JOHN. 1640. Cockermouth.
Rumper.
Third son of William. Owned Marston, Frome, Somerset, and Bushey
Park, Middlesex. Former favourite of Buckingham, then of North-
umberland. Monopoly of butter export 1619. An opportunist.[1]

HODGES, LUKE. 1646. Bristol.
Fled to Army (Percival), King's judge but refused to sign death warrant,
Rumper.
Third son of John, Shipton Mayne, Gloucester. Alderman of Bristol
1646–52, resigned. Sheriff 1638.

HOLLAND, CORNELIUS. 1641. New Windsor (see *D.N.B.*).
Fled to Army, Rumper.
Probably son of Ralph, St Lawrence Pountney, London (Venn).
Pembroke, Cambridge. Wealthy. Clerk-comptroller to Prince of
Wales. Under Vane's influence. Great gains, e.g. Creslow Manor,
Bucks., £1600–£1800 p.a. for rental of £20 p.a.[2] Bishops' land.
Puritan.

HORTON, THOMAS (see *D.N.B.*).
Regicide, war service.
Servant of Haselrig.

HOWARD, SIR EDWARD. 1649. Carlisle (see *D.N.B.*).
Rumper.
Seventh son of Thomas, 1st earl of Suffolk, but estates and title through
his mother (Lord Howard of Escrick 1628). Sinecure court office.
Expelled from Parliament for bribery 1651.

HOYLE, THOMAS. 1640. York.
Rumper.
Alderman and mayor of York 1632–3. Merchant of some wealth.[3]
Hanged himself 'in remorse' on anniversary of King's execution.[4]
Friend of John Shaw, Independent,[5] though said to be Presbyterian.[6]

HUTCHINSON, JOHN. 1646. Nottinghamshire (see *D.N.B.*).
Fled to Army, Regicide, Rumper, war service.
Son and heir of Sir Thomas, Owthorpe, Notts. Related to Ireton.
Peterhouse, Cambridge. Church lands.
Baptist.[7]

[1] M. F. Keeler, *op. cit.*   [2] *Bucks. Arch. Soc. Trans.* V, 83.
[3] M. F. Keeler, *op. cit.*
[4] *Autobiography of Alice Thornton* (Surtees Soc. vol. LXII), p. 210.
[5] *Diary of John Shaw* (Surtees Soc. vol. LXV), p. 146.
[6] *Autobiography of Alice Thornton.*
[7] Lucy Hutchinson, *Memoirs of the Life of Colonel Hutchinson,* p. 238.

INGOLDSBY, RICHARD. 1647. Wendover.
Regicide, Rumper, both Protectorate Parliaments, war service.
Second son of Sir Richard. A 'man of good extraction'.[1] Oxford and
Gray's Inn. Owned Waldrigge, Dinton, Bucks.[2] m.d. of Sir George
Crooke.[3] Related to Cromwell. Friend of Simon Mayne (q.v.).
John Wells, Independent, was his chaplain.[4]

IRETON, HENRY. 1645. Appleby (see *D.N.B.*).
Fled to Army (Percival), Regicide, Rumper, war service.
Son and heir of German of Attenborough, Notts. Trinity, Oxford and
Middle Temple. Chief theoretician of the Independents. m. Bridget
Cromwell. Refused lands and money.[5]
Religious Independent.[6]

IRETON, JOHN. 1653. London (see *D.N.B.*).
Saints' Parliament.
Second son of German of Attenborough, Notts. Clothworker and alder-
man of London 1651.
Independent, member of Cockayn's congregation.[7]

JERVOIS, SIR THOMAS. 1640. Whitchurch.
Fled to Army, Rumper, war service.
Son and heir of Thomas of Gerrar's Park, Hants. Related to Marquis of
Winchester. Wealthy, though perhaps in debt.[8] Influential.[9] Manors
of Herriard (near Wallop) through his wife, and mortgage on Steverton
and Evingar.[10] Refused loan of 1639. Sheriff of Hampshire.
Puritan[11] and probably Independent.[12]

JONES, JOHN. 1647. Merioneth (see *D.N.B.*).
Regicide, Rumper, first Protectorate Parliament, excluded from second,
war service.

[1] Clarendon, *op. cit.* XIV, § 225.
[2] *Victoria County History of Buckinghamshire*, II, 278.
[3] *Bucks. Arch. Soc. Trans.* V, 84.   [4] *C.R.*
[5] Ludlow, *op. cit.* I, 278.
[6] Woodhouse, *op. cit.*, e.g. pp. 142–3. Ireton states the classical Independent
position.
[7] *Congregational Hist. Soc. Trans.* (1933–5), p. 225.
[8] Clarendon, *op. cit.* VIII, § 129; M. F. Keeler, *op. cit.*
[9] *Cal. S. P. Dom.* (1640–1), p. 121.
[10] *Victoria County History of Hampshire*, III, 362; IV, 172, 283.
[11] M. F. Keeler, *op. cit.*
[12] Held advowson of Upper Cletford, and Independent William Hooke
was there 1627 (*C.R.*) while Independent Samuel Sprint settled there 1662
(*C.R.*).

Son of Thomas, Maesygarneth, a small Ardudwy squire. Apprenticed in London to Sir Thomas Middleton. Inherited a small freehold, had some small estates of his wife and church lands in Merioneth.[1] Opposed Protectorate until m. Cromwell's sister. Policy of security for small freeholders.[2]

Religious Independent. Friend of Vavasor Powell.

JONES, PHILIP. 1650. Brecon (see *D.N.B.*).
Rumper, Saints' Parliament, both Protectorate Parliaments, war service.
Son of David, Swansea. Alderman, 1650. Had grants of land. One of the few by-elections of Rump.

KEBLE, RICHARD.
Regicide.
Fifth son of Giles, Old Newton, Suffolk. Corpus, Cambridge and Gray's Inn. Barrister. Parliamentary Chief Justice in Wales 1648.

LASCELLES, FRANCIS. 1645. Thirsk.
Fled to Army (Percival), King's judge, but refused to sign death warrant, Rumper, Saints' Parliament, both Protectorate Parliaments, war service.
Son and heir of William of Stank, Northallerton. Gray's Inn. m.d. of Sir William St Quentin. Little activity before Pride's Purge.
Wife a convinced nonconformist.[3]

LAWRENCE, HENRY. 1646. Westmorland (see *D.N.B.*).
Purged, Saints' Parliament, both Protectorate Parliaments.
Son and heir of Sir John, St Ives, Hunts. Queens', Cambridge and Gray's Inn. Strongly against King's trial but supported Protectorate. Close friend and relative of Cromwell. Lord President of Council of State in Protectorate.
Baptist.[4]

LECHMERE, NICHOLAS. July 1648. Bewdley (see *D.N.B.*).
Rumper, both Protectorate Parliaments.
Third but surviving son of Edmund, Hanley Castle, Worcester. Wadham, Oxford and Middle Temple. Practised as lawyer. Very active in Rump.
m. fourth d. of Sir Edwin Sandys, Northbourne, Kent.

[1] A. H. Dodd, *Studies in Stuart Wales*, pp. 103 ff.
[2] *Ibid.*
[3] R. W. Dale, *History of Congregationalism in Yorkshire*, p. 144.
[4] Wrote Baptist pamphlet 1646 (*D.N.B.*).

LEMON, WILLIAM. 1645. Hertford.
>Fled to Army, refused to be King's judge, Rumper.
>Fifth son of William, Beccles, Suffolk. Sheriff of Herts. and Hunts. Woollen draper of London. Nephew of Sir John Lemon, mayor, 1631. Alderman of London nominated by Andrews and welcomed by Tichborne (q.v.). Inherited uncle's estates worth £4000 p.a. Bought Northaw Manor from Earl of Bedford.[1] Bishops' land.
>A Trier of Hertfordshire.[2] Came from Beccles, Suffolk, a centre of radical Puritanism.[3] A lay feoffee?[4]

LENTHALL, JOHN. 1645. Gloucester (see *D.N.B.*).
>Refused to be King's judge, Rumper.
>Son and heir of William (below), Wilcot and Burford, Glos. Corpus, Oxford and Lincoln's Inn.

LENTHALL, WILLIAM. 1640. Woodstock (see *D.N.B.*).
>Fled to Army, Rumper, both Protectorate Parliaments.
>Second son of William. St Alban's, Oxford and Lincoln's Inn. Barrister. Income from law, £2500 p.a.[5] Great gains from war. Speaker of House of Commons in Long Parliament.

LILBURNE, ROBERT. 1656 (see *D.N.B.*).
>Regicide, second Protectorate Parliament, war service.
>Son and heir of Richard, Thickley, Punchendon, Durham.
>Sectary.

LISLE, JOHN. 1640. Winchester (see *D.N.B.*).
>Rumper, both Protectorate Parliaments.
>Second son of Sir William, Moyles Court, Hants. Magdalen Hall, Oxford. Barrister. Friend of Cromwell. Very active in Parliament. Moderately wealthy.[6]
>Religious Independent,[7] noted for devotion.

LISLE, LORD PHILIP. 1640. Yarmouth, Isle of Wight (see *D.N.B.*).
>Fled to Army, refused to be King's judge, Rumper, Saints' Parliament, both Protectorate Parliaments.
>Son and heir of Robert, 2nd Earl of Leicester. Said to inherit £1500 p.a. on his marriage.[8] War service in Ireland. Active support of Republic.
>Puritan. Independent?

[1] Brunton and Pennington, *op. cit.* p. 119; *V.C.H. Herts.* II, 358.
[2] W. Urwick, *Nonconformity in Hertfordshire*, p. 834.
[3] H. J. Hosken, *History of the Congregational Churches of Suffolk*, p. 198.
[4] Rushworth, *op. cit.* II, 150.
[5] *Notes and Queries*, I, xii, 358.   [6] M. F. Keeler, *op. cit.*
[7] *Congregational Hist. Soc. Trans.* VII, 280.
[8] M. F. Keeler, *op. cit.*

Appendix A

LISTER, THOMAS. 1647. Lincoln (see *D.N.B.*).
Fled to Army, King's judge but refused to sign death warrant, Rumper, first Protectorate Parliament, excluded from second, war service.
Son and heir of William of Coleby Hall, Lincs. Old respected family. Estates. Gray's Inn. m.d. of Sir William Armine. Active in Parliament.

LIVESEY, MICHAEL. 1645. Queensborough (see *D.N.B.*).
Fled to Army, Regicide, Rumper.
Son and heir of Gabriel, Hollingbourne, Kent. Also with manor at East Church. Great local influence. Exempted from pardon, 1642. Extravagant debauchee.[1] Great gains from war.

LONG, LISLEBONE. 1647. Wells (see *D.N.B.*).
Rumper, both Protectorate Parliaments.
Son and heir of William, Stratton-on-Fosse, Somerset. Magdalen Hall, Oxford and Lincoln's Inn. 'A sober, good and discreet lawyer.'[2] Many important posts under Cromwell.[3] Bishops' land.
Presbyterian elder.[4]

LOVE, NICHOLAS. 1645. Winchester (see *D.N.B.*).
Fled to Army, King's judge but refused to sign death warrant, Rumper.
Son and heir of Nicholas, warden of Winchester College and formerly chaplain to James I. Wadham, Oxford and Lincoln's Inn. Lawyer and financier. Royalist lands and financial posts.

LUDLOW, EDMUND. 1645. Wiltshire (see *D.N.B.*).
Fled to Army, Regicide, Rumper, war service.
Son of Sir Henry, Marden, Bradley, Wilts. Father radical. Oxford and Inner Temple. Extreme Republican. In Ireland. A chief promoter of Pride's Purge. Bishops' lands. Refused to recognize Cromwell.
Sectary?[5]

MACKWORTH, THOMAS. 1646. Ludlow.
Purged Rumper.
Son and heir of Col. Humphrey of Betton, Shropshire, Governor of Shrewsbury, who served in the Protectorate Parliaments and was a strong Puritan.[6] Fined for non-attendance at Rump. Tended to royalism.

---

[1] Noble, *op. cit.*
[2] Whitelocke, quoted in *D.N.B.*   [3] Harbin, *op. cit.* p. 166.
[4] Shaw, *op. cit.* II, 417.
[5] From his memoirs, obviously a keen Puritan. According to Baxter, the leader of the Anabaptists in Ireland (*Reliquae Baxterianae*, I, 74).
[6] Baxter, *op. cit.* I, 44.

MALOVERS, THOMAS. 1640. Boroughbridge (see *D.N.B.*).
Regicide, Rumper, war service.
Son and heir of Sir Richard, High Sheriff of York. Estates in Yorks worth
£1500 p.a.[1] St John's, Cambridge and Gray's Inn. Very strong
Parliamentarian, but son a Royalist. His d.m. Thomas Scott.

MARTEN, HENRY. 1640. Berkshire (see *D.N.B.*).
Fled to Army, Regicide, Rumper.
Son of Sir Henry. Probably self-made man. Judge of the Admiralty and
member of High Commission. Protégé of Archbishop Abbot.
University College, Oxford and Inner Temple. Inherited estates of
£3000–£4000 p.a. By 1660 debts were over £50,000. m. sister of
Lord Lovelace. His d.m. Lord Morley and Monteagle. Friend of
Wildman, Walwyn, Lilburne, Thomas Chaloner, Henry Nevil and
Sir Henry Ludlow.[2]
Theist.

MASHAM, SIR WILLIAM. 1640. Essex.
Refused to be King's judge. Rumper.
Son of William, Otes, Essex. Well-established family. Baronet 1621.
Bought High Laver manor.[3] m.d. of Sir Francis Barrington, widow
of Sir James Altham, Mark Hall in Latton. Magdalen, Oxford and
Inner Temple. In opposition to Crown 1626.
Presbyterian elder[4] but Roger Williams was his chaplain 1633[5] and
Owen, a leading Independent, dedicated his book *Ebenezer* to him,
1648.

MASHAM, WILLIAM. 1646. Shrewsbury.
Rumper, first Protectorate Parliament.
Son and heir of above. St Catharine's, Cambridge. m.d. of Sir John
Trevor. Sister m. Oliver St John (q.v). Cousin of Cromwell. Active
in Parliament.[6] Bishops' land.
Presbyterian elder, but Independent, Henry Lukin, was chaplain to the
family after 1660.[7]

---

[1] M. F. Keeler, *op. cit.*
[2] I am indebted to Dr C. M. Williams, who has recently made an intensive
study of Henry Marten, for information on this subject.
[3] Brunton and Pennington, *op. cit.* pp. 120–1; Morant, *History of Essex*, II,
141.
[4] Shaw, *op. cit.* II, 380.
[5] *Congregational Hist. Soc. Trans.* IX, 263.
[6] *Essex Arch. Soc. Trans.* II, 27; *Shropshire Arch. Soc. Trans.* XII, 212.
[7] Shaw, *op. cit.*; *C.R.*

Appendix A

MAYNE, SIMON. 1645. Aylesbury (see *D.N.B.*).
Fled to Army, Regicide, Rumper (entered dissent 25 Dec. 1648).
Son and heir of Simon, Dinton Hall, nr. Aylesbury, 'very ancient family, considerable estate and a person of importance'.[1] Friend of Ingoldsby (q.v.).
Held advowson of Dinton, which he offered to Seth Wood the Independent.[2]

MILDMAY, SIR HENRY. 1640. Maldon (see *D.N.B.*).
Fled to Army, King's judge but refused to sign death warrant, Rumper, first Protectorate Parliament, excluded from second.
Younger son of Sir Humphrey, Danbury Place, Essex. Emmanuel, Cambridge, and Gray's Inn. Brought up at Court and raised to high offices and estates (e.g. Wanstead, Essex, worth £1000 p.a.) by James and Charles, yet in debt.[3] Great gains from war. Notorious peculation.
Presbyterian elder, but installed L. Hoar, a Congregationalist in 1656[4] and sent his son to Harvard 1644 'to receive true doctrine'.[5]

MILLINGTON, GILBERT. 1646. Nottingham (see *D.N.B.*).
Regicide, Rumper.
Son and heir of Anthony, Felley Abbey, Notts, worth £200 p.a.[6] Lesser gentry.[7] Peterhouse, Cambridge and Lincoln's Inn. Called to bar 1621.
Called an Independent by Walker.[8] Fifth Monarchist?[9]

MONSON, LORD WILLIAM. 1640. Reigate (see *D.N.B.*).
Fled to Army, King's judge but refused to sign death warrant, Rumper.
Second son but heir of Admiral Sir William, Kennersley, and Margaret, d. of Sir Edward Anderson. Lord Chief Justice of Common Pleas. Gray's Inn. Attempt made to make him James I's favourite. Peer 1628. Royalist until 1646. Estates in Reigate, Surrey, from first wife, but dissolute and soon in debt. Imprisoned for debt 1659.[10]

[1] Noble, *op. cit.*   [2] *C.R.*
[3] Clarendon, *op. cit.* XI, § 237; M. F. Keeler, *op. cit.*   [4] *C.R.*
[5] W. L. Sachse, *op. cit.*; *American Hist. Rev.* LIII, 261.
[6] M. F. Keeler, *op. cit.*
[7] A. C. Wood, *Nottinghamshire in the Great Civil War*, p. 34.
[8] Walker, *op. cit.* I, 81.
[9] *Clarendon State Papers*, March 1653, quoted in *English Historical Review* (1893), p. 529.
[10] Brayley and Britten, *Surrey*, IV, 219–23.

MOORE, JOHN. 1640. Liverpool.
> Survived Purge. Regicide, d. 1650, war service.
> Son and heir of Edward, Bank Hall, nr. Liverpool. The only Protestant gentleman in the neighbourhood. Mayor of Liverpool 1633. Very active in war and Parliament. Left debts of £10,000 though probably wealthy when war broke out.[1]
> Presbyterian elder.[2]

MORICE, WILLIAM. 1648. Devon (see *D.N.B.*).
> Rumper, first Protectorate Parliament, excluded from second.
> Son and heir of John, Chancellor of Exeter. Exeter, Oxford. J.P. and sheriff of Devon.
> Helped William Oliver, an ejected minister.[3]

MORLEY, HERBERT. 1640. Lewes (see *D.N.B.*).
> Fled to Army (Percival), King's judge but refused to sign death warrant, Rumper, first Protectorate Parliament, excluded from second, war service.
> Son and heir of Robert, Glynde, Sussex, a royal ward.[4] Emmanuel, Cambridge and Inner Temple. One of leading men of county, with great local influence. Son m.d. of Sir John Trevor.[5] Very active for Parliament.
> Strong Puritan. Helped ejected and radical clergy.[6]

MOYER, SAMUEL. 1653. London.
> Saints' Parliament.
> London financier. Member of East India Company. Bishops' land.
> Baptist.[7]

MOYLE, JOHN. 1648. E. Looe (see *D.N.B.*).
> Rumper.
> Son and heir of Robert, Bake, Cornwall. Exeter, Oxford. Sheriff of Cornwall 1624. Friend of Eliot. m.d. of Sir Edmund Prideaux.

NELTHROP, JAMES. 1645. Beverley.
> Refused to be King's judge, Rumper.
> A younger son. Mercer of Beverley and mayor 1641. Bishops' land (?).

---

[1] *The Moore Rental* (Chetham Soc. vol. XII), p. 56; M. F. Keeler, *op. cit.*
[2] Shaw, *op. cit.* II, 415.
[3] C.R.   [4] M. F. Keeler, *op. cit.*
[5] *Sussex Arch. Soc. Trans.* V, 91.
[6] C.R., under N. Beaton and Z. Smith.
[7] L. Brown, *op. cit.* p. 10.

Appendix A

NEVIL, HENRY. Oct. 1649. Abingdon (see *D.N.B.*).
Rumper.
Second son of Sir Henry of Billinghere, Werfield, Bucks. Merton, Oxford. m.d. of Richard Staverton. Friend of Marten and Challoner. Very active in Rump.
Theist.

NICHOLAS, ROBERT. 1640. Devizes (see *D.N.B.*).
Refused to be King's judge, Rumper.
Son of John, of Devizes and Roundway, Wilts. Queen's, Oxford and Inner Temple. Lawyer of Devizes. m.d. of Sir Thos. Broderick. Reputedly assisted to draw up charge against Charles. Lesser Gentry.[1]

NOEL, MARTIN. 1656. Stafford.
Second Protectorate Parliament.
Of Stafford and London. Thurloe's brother-in-law. Great capitalist shipowner and money-lender. Colonizing activity.[2] London Alderman, 1657.[3]
'A person of devotion.'[4]

NORTON, SIR GREGORY. 1645. Midhurst.
Fled to Army, Regicide, Rumper.
Second son but heir of Henry (but see Noble, *op. cit.*). Estates in Sussex; Hants; Charlton, Berks and Hempden, Bucks. m.d. of Bradshaw. Gains from war.[5]

NUTT, JOHN. 1640. Canterbury.
Refused to be King's judge, Rumper.
Son and heir of William, lawyer of Canterbury. Exeter, Oxford and Middle Temple. Bishops' land though probably not wealthy.[6]

OKEY, JOHN. 1654. Perth (see *D.N.B.*).
Regicide, first Protectorate Parliament, war service.
Father said to be of Brogborough, Beds, and a friend of Edmund Dell, Master of Caius, Cambridge. Lilburne refers to him as a tool of the Independents.[7]
Independent[8] and Fifth Monarchist.

---

[1] M. F. Keeler, *op. cit.*   [2] A. P. Newton, *op. cit.* p. 325.
[3] *Staffs. Hist. Soc. Trans.* (1922), p. 103.
[4] *Ibid.*
[5] *Victoria County History of Buckinghamshire*, III, 328; Noble, *op. cit.*; and *Sussex Arch. Soc. Trans.* v, 90 for evidence on this elusive character.
[6] M. F. Keeler, *op. cit.*
[7] 'Legal Fundamental Liberties', in Woodhouse, *op. cit.* p. 349.
[8] Woodhouse, *op. cit.* pp. 349, 467.

OLDSWORTH, MICHAEL. 1640. Old Sarum (see *D.N.B.*).
Rumper.
Son of Arnold, Bradley, Gloucester. Queen's and Magdalen, Oxford.
Estates from Charles, e.g. Sandridge, Kent. Secretary to Earl of
Pembroke, whom he influenced greatly.

PALMER, JOHN. 1644. Taunton.
Rumper, war service.
Son of a Taunton apothecary, Queen's, Oxford.
Presbyterian elder.[1]

PARKER, HENRY (see *D.N.B.*).
Fourth son of Sir Nicholas, Sussex. St Edmund Hall, Oxford and
Lincoln's Inn. Secretarial posts with Merchant Adventurers, Army
and Commonwealth. Republican theoretician.
Presbyterian, then Erastian Independent.[2]

PELHAM, PEREGRINE. 1640. Hull.
Regicide, Rumper, d. 1650.
Son and heir of Peregrine and grandson of Sir William, Brockesley, Lincs.
Many estates, Wickham, Rothwell, Normandy, Claxby, Kelebie and
Croxton. Alderman and mayor of Hull. A merchant of some local
importance.[3]

PENNINGTON, ISAAC. 1640. London (see *D.N.B.*).
King's judge but refused to sign death warrant, Rumper.
Son and heir of Robert, London merchant. Very rich. Estates in East
Anglia, and Bucks. 'Ran' the City radicals.
Independent. Member of John Goodwin's congregation.

PICKERING, SIR GILBERT. 1640. Northants (see *D.N.B.*).
King's judge but refused to sign death warrant, Rumper, Saints' Parlia-
ment, both Protectorate Parliaments, war service.
Son and heir of Sir John, Tidmarsh, Northants. Several other manors.[4]
Emmanuel, Cambridge and Gray's Inn. m. (i) d. of Sir Sidney
Montague, Hinchingbrooke, Hunts; (ii) d. of John Pepys, Cottenham,
Cambridge. One of Cromwell's peers.
Presbyterian, then Independent, then sectary.

PIERPOINT, WILLIAM. 1640. Much Wenlock (see *D.N.B.*).
Fled to Army, Purged, first Protectorate Parliament.
Second son of Robert, 1st Earl of Kingston, a 'man of vast estate'.[5]
Emmanuel, Cambridge and Lincoln's Inn. m.d. of Sir Thomas Harris

[1] Shaw, *op. cit.* II, 42.
[2] W. K. Jordan, *Men of Substance*, gives a very good account of Parker.
[3] Noble, *op. cit.*; M. F. Keeler, *op. cit.*
[4] Bridges, *History of Northants*, II, 383.   [5] Lucy Hutchinson, *op. cit.* p. 93.

and acquired the Tonge estates. £7467 from his brother Henry's composition and £10,000 from his father's estate.[1] Great learning and moderation. Much royalist land. At first in peace party, but after 1645 sided with war party until Pride's Purge.[2]
Moderate Puritan.

PIGGOTTS, GERVASE. 1645. Notts.
Fled to Army, Purged, Rumper.
Son and heir of Gervase, Thrumpton, Notts. St Catharine's, Cambridge. Related to Thornaugh. m.d. of John Bradshaw. Lesser gentry.[3]
Strong Puritan. 'A man of piety.'[4]

POPHAM, ALEXANDER. 1640. Bath.
Rumper, first Protectorate Parliament, excluded from second, war service.
Second son but heir of Sir Francis, Littlecote, Somerset. Balliol, Oxford. Inherited estates of £10,000 p.a. in 1638 but possibly wasted them.[5] Clarendon describes his father as being 'of the Independent party'.[6] Active in raising troops for Parliament. One of Cromwell's peers.

POTTER, VINCENT.
Regicide, Colonel.
Returned from New England to serve in Army.[7]

PRIDE, THOMAS. 1656. Reigate (see *D.N.B.*).
Regicide, second Protectorate Parliament, war service.
Origins obscure. Magdalen Hall, Oxford and Gray's Inn. Worcester House, Malden, Surrey.

PRIDEAUX, EDMUND. 1640. Lyme Regis (see *D.N.B.*).
Fled to Army, refused to be King's judge, Rumper, both Protectorate Parliaments.
Second son of Sir Edward. Inner Temple. Lawyer of Ford Abbey, Dorset. Linked by Clarendon with Vane and St John.[8]
Presbyterian elder[9] but son was certainly, and he probably, Congregationalist. Nonconformist services held at Ford Abbey.[10]

---

[1] *Shropshire Arch. Soc. Trans.* (1928), p. 169.
[2] Clarendon, *op. cit.* VIII, § 240.
[3] Wood, *op. cit.* p. 34; Thornton, *History of Nottinghamshire*, I, 33.
[4] Lucy Hutchinson, *op. cit.* p. 108.
[5] Aubrey, *Brief Lives* (1949 ed.), p. 184.
[6] Clarendon, *op. cit.* VIII, § 240.   [7] W. L. Sachse, *op. cit.* p. 274.
[8] Clarendon, *op. cit.* VIII, § 241.   [9] Shaw, *op. cit.* II, 404.
[10] W. Densham and J. Ogle, *The Story of Congregational Churches in Dorset*, p. 9.

PUREFOY, WILLIAM. 1640. Warwick (see *D.N.B.*).
Fled to Army, Regicide, Rumper, both Protectorate Parliaments, war service.
Son and heir of Francis, Caldecote, Warwick. Emmanuel, Cambridge, and Gray's Inn. Good landed estate. 'Bore great sway in his native county.'[1] Strong republican after visit to Geneva.[2] Friend of Lord Brooke.
Strong Puritan. Fifth Monarchist?[3]

PUREY, THOMAS. 1640. Gloucester.
Rumper, first Protectorate Parliament, war service.
Son of Walter, clothier, of Gloucester. Manors of Taynton and Minster,[4] but probably not wealthy.[5] Alderman and mayor 1643.
Strong Puritan, and attacked episcopacy in Root and Branch debate.[6] Called an Independent by Walker.[7]

PUREY, THOMAS, JR. 1646. Monmouth.
Rumper, second Protectorate Parliament.
Son of above.
Called an Independent by Walker.[8]

PYNE, JOHN. 1640. Poole.
Rumper, Saints' Parliament, war service.
Son of Thomas, Curry Mallett, Somerset. Grandfather's heir. 'A gentleman well known and of fair estate in that county.'[9] Income probably £2000 p.a.[10] 1638 protested against ship money. Disapproved of King's trial but supported Commonwealth.[11]
Presbyterian elder[12] but friendly to Quakers.[13]

RADCLIFFE, JOHN. 1645. Chester.
Rumper.
Son of John, Alderman of Chester. Queen's, Oxford and Middle Temple. Alderman and Recorder of Chester. Friend of Bradshaw.
Nonconformist? In 1661 had not taken the sacrament for a year.[14]

---

[1] Nichols, *op. cit.* IV, 602.
[2] T. M. Whitley, *Parliamentary Representation of the City of Coventry*, p. 91.
[3] *Clarendon State Papers*, in *English Hist. Rev.* (1893), p. 529.
[4] *Bristol and Gloucester Arch. Soc. Trans.* XLIII, 178.
[5] M. F. Keeler, *op. cit.*
[6] *Ibid.*; Rushworth, *op. cit.* III, 289–91.
[7] Walker, *op. cit.* I, 81.   [8] *Ibid.*
[9] Clarendon, *op. cit.* VIII, § 240.   [10] M. F. Keeler, *op. cit.*
[11] Harbin, *op. cit.* p. 153.   [12] Shaw, *op. cit.* II, 421.
[13] *Extracts from State Papers relating to Friends* (ed. N. Penney), index.
[14] W. D. Pink MSS.

Appendix A

REYNOLDS, SIR ROBERT. 1640. Hindon (see *D.N.B.*).
Refused to be King's judge, Rumper.
Son and heir of Sir James, Castle Camps, Cambridge. Queens', Cambridge and Middle Temple. Younger brother, Sir John, was active for Parliament and radical. At first Presbyterian but 'is since fallen off and become thoroughly theirs' (Holles).[1] Much bishops' land gained. Solicitor-General 1650. Dropped out of affairs after 1653, until the death of Cromwell. Probably wealthy.
Presbyterian elder.[2] Member of Westminster Assembly. Certainly not a Presbyterian, probably Erastian.[3]

RICH, NATHANIEL. 1649. Cirencester (see *D.N.B.*).
Rumper, war service.
Son and heir of Robert. Inherited Essex estates of uncle Nathaniel, son of 1st Baron Rich. St Catharine's, Cambridge and Gray's Inn. Republican and very active in Army. Helped draw up Independent 'Heads of Proposals'.
For religious toleration.[4] Fifth Monarchist?[5]

RIGBY, ALEXANDER. 1640. Wigan (see *D.N.B.*).
Refused to be King's judge, Rumper, war service. d. 1650.
Son and heir of Alexander, Middleton, nr. Preston, Lancs. St John's, Cambridge and Gray's Inn. Lawyer. Very active for Parliament. Appointed Baron of Exchequer by Cromwell.[6] Reputed to be wealthy.[7]
Presbyterian elder.[8] Became Independent, according to Vicars.[9]

ROBINSON, LUKE. 1645. Scarborough.
Rumper, both Protectorate Parliaments.
Son and heir of Sir Arthur, Deighton, Yorks. Christ's, Cambridge and Gray's Inn. Very active in Parliament.[10]
Extreme Puritan. Friendly to Quakers.[11]

---

[1] Holles, *op. cit.* in Maseres, *Tracts*, I, 308.
[2] Shaw, *op. cit.* II, 428.   [3] Burton, *op. cit.* III, 208–9.
[4] Woodhouse, *op. cit.* pp. 128, 149.
[5] *Clarendon State Papers*, in *English Hist. Rev.* (1893), p. 529 and Ludlow, I, 345.
[6] E. Broxap, *Lancashire and the Great Civil War*, p. 33.
[7] M. F. Keeler, *op. cit.*   [8] Shaw, *op. cit.* II, 397.
[9] J. Vicars, *Dagon Demolished* (1660), 'A most desperate enemy of the Presbyterian church system'.
[10] *Yorks. Arch. Assoc. Trans.* (1938), p. 80.
[11] Burton, *op. cit.* I, 228; Fox, *op. cit.* I, 26.

ROGERS, HUGH CALNE. 1640.
Possibly purged, readmitted Nov. 1650, Rumper, war service.
Son and heir of Sir Francis, Cannington, Somerset. Hart Hall, Oxford.
m.d. of Sir Edward Bainton (q.v.). Thirteen manors in Somerset, two
in Cornwall, one in Wilts.[1]

ROUS, FRANCIS. 1640. Truro (see *D.N.B.*).
Fled to Army (Percival), Rumper, Saints' and both Protectorate
Parliaments.
Son and heir of Sir Anthony, Halton, nr. Saltash, Cornwall. Stepbrother
of Pym. Speaker in Saints' Parliament.
In Westminster Assembly. Conservative but mystical type of Puritan.

ROWE, OWEN (see *D.N.B.*).
Regicide.
Yeoman's son, Bickley, Cheshire. London merchant. m.d. of Thomas
Scott.[2] Supported Independents against Levellers.[3] Colonizing
companies.
Independent of St Stephen's, Coleman St. Fifth Monarchist.

SALWAY, HUMPHREY. 1640. Worcestershire (see *D.N.B.*).
Fled to Army (Percival), survived Purge, refused to be King's judge,
d. 1652.
Son and heir of Arthur, Stanford, Worcester. Brasenose, Oxford and
Inner Temple. Held manor of Stanford-on-Teme and advowson.[4]
m.d. of Sir Edward Lyttleton, Pellaton Hall, Staffs. King's Re-
membrancer of Exchequer, £400 p.a.[5] Probably wealthy.[6] Fined for
distraint of knighthood.
Lay member of Westminster Assembly.

SALWAY, RICHARD. 1645. Appleby (see *D.N.B.*).
Fled to Army (Percival), refused to be King's judge, Rumper, Saints'
Parliament, war service.
Fourth son of Humphrey, above. Inner Temple. Of Richard's Castle,
Shropshire, and merchant of London. Mayor of Worcester. m.d. of
Alderman Richard Waring, London. £1000 p.a. as Commissioner in
Ireland, 1650. Much bishops' and royalist land gained. 'A man of
great parts.'[7]
Adherent of Vane in religion.[8]

---

[1] M. F. Keeler, *op. cit.*
[2] *Bucks. Arch. Soc. Trans.* v, 89.
[3] Woodhouse, *op. cit.* p. 349.
[4] *V.C.H. Worcestershire*, IV, 342.
[5] W. R. Williams, *Members for Worcester*, p. 42.
[6] M. F. Keeler, *op. cit.*
[7] Williams, *op. cit.* p. 43; H. A. Glass, *The Barebones Parliament*, p. 84.
[8] Baxter, *Reliquae Baxterianae*, I, 63.

Appendix A

SAY, WILLIAM. 1647. Camelford (see *D.N.B.*).
Regicide, Rumper.
Second son of William of Ickenham, Middlesex. Ancient family.
Estates in Fens. University College, Oxford and Middle Temple.
Lawyer. Active in Parliament.

SCOTT, THOMAS. 1645. Aylesbury (see *D.N.B.*).
Fled to Army, Regicide, Rumper. First Protectorate Parliament, excluded
from second.
Origins obscure. Son of Joshua, Hull (?). Cambridge?[1] m.d. of Allanson
and/or Malovers and/or Packington, Aylesbury. Apparently related to
Scott family in Kent. Consistently Republican. Bishops' lands.
Probably Independent. Related to Independents at Canterbury?[2] Puritan
language at execution consistent with Independency,[3] and in Parliament 1658, talked about God governing his church by plain things and
low things.[4]

SCROPE, ADRIAN (see *D.N.B.*).
Regicide, war service.
Son and heir of Robert, Wormsby, Oxford. Hart Hall, Oxford and
Middle Temple. Active and radical in Army. Unrepenting Regicide.
Church meeting at his house.[5] Puritan language at execution.[6]

SERLE, GEORGE. 1640. Taunton.
Rumper.
Christ Church, Oxford and Lincoln's Inn.[7] Lawyer. Mayor of Taunton.
Presbyterian elder.[8]

SKINNER, AUGUSTINE. 1642. Kent (see *D.N.B.*).
Fled to Army, refused to be King's judge, Rumper, first Protectorate
Parliament, war service.
Son of Augustine, London merchant. Of Lincolnshire family recently
settled at Totesham Hall, East Farleigh, Kent. Balliol, Oxford and
Middle Temple. Bishops' land.
Strong Puritan. Said he was no Separatist. Like the Independents he
wanted lay patrons retained but more rights to the congregation.[9]

[1] Venn.
[2] *Congregational Hist. Soc. Trans.* VII, 264.
[3] Howell, *op. cit.* v, 1272 ff.   [4] Burton, *op. cit.* II, 389.
[5] M. Caston, *Independency at Bristol*, p. 41.
[6] Howell, *op. cit.* v, 1272 ff.   [7] M. F. Keeler, *op. cit.*
[8] Shaw, *op. cit.* II, 420.
[9] Stowe MSS. (B.M.), 744–13. I am indebted to Mr Alan Everitt of the
University of London for this and other information about the Kentish
families.

SKIPPON, PHILIP. 1646. Barnstaple (see *D.N.B.*).
Fled to Army (Percival), refused to be King's judge, Rumper, both Protectorate Parliaments, war service.
Son and heir of Luke, Foulsham, Norfolk. Inherited uncle's estates. Conservative Independent, both politically and religiously. Bishops' land.
Puritan. Wrote devotional works.[1] Richard Worts was Independent vicar of Foulsham.[2] Anti-Naylor.[3]

SMITH, HENRY. 1645. Leicestershire (see *D.N.B.*).
Fled to Army, Regicide, Rumper.
Son and heir of Henry, Withcote, Leicester. Manor of 900 acres, £600 p.a.[4] Magdalen, Oxford and Lincoln's Inn, 'a lawyer but a mean one'.[5] Related to Henry Smith, leading Elizabethan Puritan.[6]

SMITH, PHILIP. 1641. Southwark.
Fled to Army, Rumper.
Son and heir of Henry, Haydon Modhouse, Cherney, Wilts. Inner Temple. Probably not wealthy.[7]

SNELLING, GEORGE. 1645. Southwark.
Survived Purge.
Either second son of John of Chandlewood *or* of Thistlewood, Middlesex. Presbyterian elder[8] of St Olave's, Southwark.

ST JOHN, OLIVER. 1640. Totnes (see *D.N.B.*).
Fled to Army, Rumper.
Son and heir of Oliver, Caystoe, Bedfordshire. Queens', Cambridge and Lincoln's Inn. Colonizing activity with Pym. Leading Independent with Vane in Parliament until end of 1648. Income probably less than £200 p.a. in 1630.[9]
Puritan.[10] m.d. of leading Independent minister J. Oxenbridge.[11] Erastian.

STAPLETON, BRIAN. 1645. Aldborough.
Survived Purge.
Son and heir of Sir Robert, Myton, nr. Boroughbridge, Yorks. Receiver-General for Charles I. m.d. of Sir Henry Slingsby, royalist.[12]

---

[1] *Congregational Hist. Soc. Trans.* vol. IV.
[2] *C.R.*   [3] Burton, *op. cit.* I, 48.
[4] *Reports and Papers of Associated Archaeological Societies* (1922), pp. 147 ff.
[5] Heath, *Chronicle*, p. 200.   [6] *Reports and Papers.*
[7] M. F. Keeler, *op. cit.*   [8] Shaw, *op. cit.* II, 403.
[9] M. F. Keeler, *op. cit.*   [10] *Thurloe State Papers*, I, 75.   [11] *C.R.*
[12] Venn lists him as a member of Sidney Sussex, Cambridge, but I think misidentifies him. See Thomas Lawson-Tancred, *Records of a Yorkshire Manor*, p. 376.

STAPLEY, ANTONY. 1640. Sussex (see *D.N.B.*).
Regicide, Rumper, Saints' Parliament. Both Protectorate Parliaments, war service.
Son of Anthony, Patcham, Sussex. For a time, ward of the Crown.[1] Christ's, Cambridge and Gray's Inn. Probably wealthy.[2] m.d. of Lord Goring. Lucrative posts under Protectorate.[3]
Puritan in opposition to Laud.[4] Son helped ejected nonconformists.[5]

STEELE, WILLIAM. 1654. New Romney (see *D.N.B.*).
First Protectorate Parliament.
Son of Richard, Sandbach Hall, Cheshire. Caius, Cambridge and Gray's Inn. Lawyer. Recorder of London. Lord Chancellor of Ireland, 1656. Active lawyer for Rump and Protectorate.
Baptist.[6]

STRICKLAND, WALTER. 1646. Minehead (see *D.N.B.*).
Rumper, Saints' Parliament, both Protectorate Parliaments.
Son of Walter of Boynton, brother of 1st Baronet Boynton. Queens', Cambridge and Gray's Inn. Lawyer. Ambassador to Holland, 1642–8.
Strict Puritan.[7] John Shaw, Independent, dedicated a book to his wife.[8]

STRICKLAND, SIR WILLIAM. 1640. Hedon (see *D.N.B.*).
Rumper, both Protectorate Parliaments.
Elder brother of above. Queens', Cambridge and Gray's Inn. Nine manors worth £1500–£2000 p.a. in Yorkshire.[9]

STOCKDALE, THOMAS. 1645. Knaresborough.
Rumper, d. 1653.
Son of William, Betton Park, Yorkshire.

SYDENHAM, WILLIAM. 1645. Weymouth (see *D.N.B.*).
Rumper, Saints' Parliament, both Protectorate Parliaments, war service.
Of Wingfield Eagle, Dorset. Trinity, Oxford. Active in war and in Cromwellian Parliaments.
Independent. Owen's congregation.[10]

---

[1] M. F. Keeler, *op. cit.*   [2] *Ibid.*
[3] C. Thomas-Stanford, *op. cit.* p. 227.
[4] M. F. Keeler, *op. cit.*   [5] *C.R.* under William Wallace.
[6] L. Brown, *op. cit.* p. 10.   [7] Burton, *op. cit.* I, 229.
[8] *Diary of John Shaw* (Surtees Soc., vol. LXV), p. 431.
[9] M. F. Keeler, *op. cit.*
[10] Lansdowne MSS. (B.M.), folios 823–251.

SYDNEY, ALGERNON. 1646. Cardiff (see *D.N.B.*).
Fled to Army (Percival), refused to be King's judge, Rumper.
Second son of Earl of Leicester. Bemoaned lack of estates. Republican, but against King's trial for legal reasons. Friend of Wildman and Slingsby Bethel.
Devotional works.

TEMPLE, JAMES. 1645. Bramber (see *D.N.B.*).
Fled to Army, Regicide, Rumper, war service. Probably son and heir of Alexander, Etchingham, Sussex.
Cousin of Sir Peter. Repentant Regicide.

TEMPLE, SIR PETER. 1640. Buckingham (see *D.N.B.*).
Fled to Army? Survived Purge? Refused to be King's judge, Rumper.
Son and heir of Sir Thomas, Stowe, Bucks. Eminent family but indebted in seventeenth century. 1647 debts £20,000. 1651 income £3500. Law suits. Took no part in Parliament after King's trial, though entered his dissent Feb. 1649. On only one Rump committee.
No evidence of any religious radicalism. Son a member of Peter Grinning's congregation, consistently Anglican.[1]

TEMPLE, PETER. 1645. Leicester (see *D.N.B.*).
Fled to Army? Survived Purge? Regicide, Rumper, war service.
Third son but heir of Edmund Temple, Temple Hall, Sibbesdon, Leicester. Cousin of above. m.d. of Robert Burgoine, Wroxall, Warwick. High Sheriff of Leicester, 1644. £1500 voted to him.[2]

THOMSON, GEORGE. 1645. Southwark (see *D.N.B.*).
Rumper, war service.
Either son of Thomas, London (Pink), or of Robert, Herts. London merchant. Uncle of Lord Haversham. Bishops' land.
Presbyterian elder at St Olave's, Southwark.[3] Later Fifth Monarchist.

THORNAUGH, FRANCIS. 1646. Retford.
Fled to Army, war service, killed 1648.
Son and heir of Sir Francis, Fenton, Notts. Magdalen, Oxford and Inner Temple. Sheriff of Notts. Very influential in county.[4]
Very strong Puritan.[5]

THORPE, FRANCIS. 1645. Richmond (see *D.N.B.*).
Refused to be King's judge, Rumper, first Protectorate Parliament, excluded from second, war service.

[1] *Huntington Library Quarterly*, vols. II, IV, for article on the Temple family.
[2] Nichols, *op. cit.* I, 461; III, 433; IV, 959.
[3] Shaw, *op. cit.* II, 403.   [4] Wood, *op. cit.* p. 34.
[5] Hutchinson, *op. cit.* p. 108.

Son and heir of Roger, Birdsall, Yorkshire. St John's, Cambridge and Gray's Inn. Lawyer. Recorder of Beverley, 1623, and of Hull, 1639. Pro-Republican, opposed to Cromwell.[1]

Sectary. Related to Saltmarsh, and friend of Hotham, who published Boehme's works.

TICHBORNE, ROBERT. 1653. London (see *D.N.B.*).

Regicide, Saints' Parliament, in Cromwell's Upper House.

Linen draper of Cheapside. Captain in London Trained Bands. Republican. Lord Mayor of London, 1656. Gains from war. Bishops' lands.

Independent.[2] Wrote on religious experience.

TOLL, THOMAS. 1640. King's Lynn.

Rumper, Saints' Parliament.

Eldest son of rector of Wells. Alderman and Mayor of Lynn, 1639 and 1646. m.d. of Thomas Soames, Mayor of Lynn.[3] Probably not wealthy but owned property in Lynn.[4]

TRENCHARD, JOHN. 1645. Wareham.

Fled to Army, refused to be King's judge, Rumper, both Protectorate Parliaments.

Very ancient Dorset family. Daughters m. Bingham and Sydenham (q.v.). Much royalist land.[5]

Trenchard family helped ejected clergy.[6]

TREVOR, SIR JOHN. 1640. Grampound.

Fled to Army (Percival), Rumper, both Protectorate Parliaments.

Son and heir of Sir John, Oatlands, Surrey and Trevallyn, Denbigh. Queens', Cambridge and Inner Temple. Very rich. Part-owner of Newcastle coal monopoly £1200–£1500 p.a. Great gains in war. m.d. of John Hampden. His d. m. son of Morley.

On 'Gospel in Wales' Committee, 1654.[7]

---

[1] Burton, *op. cit* II, 445.

[2] Member of Cockayn's Independent Church. Calamy, *Continuation of Account*, p. 51.

[3] Brunton and Pennington, *op. cit.* pp. 78–9.

[4] M. F. Keeler, *op. cit.*

[5] Brunton and Pennington, *op. cit.* pp. 160, 172.

[6] *C.R.* under Samuel Hardy and Thomas Rowe.

[7] For Trevor see: *Sussex Arch. Soc. Trans.* v, 94; Lipscombe, *History of Buckinghamshire*, II, 297; *Surrey Arch. Soc. Collection*, XVII, 47; and M. F. Keeler, *op. cit.*

VALENTINE, BENJAMIN. 1640. St Germans (see *D.N.B.*).
Rumper, d. 1653.
Probably from Cheshire. With Holles, held Speaker Finch in chair.
Imprisoned and fined by Charles. Not very active in Parliament.
Probably not rich.[1]

VANE, SIR HENRY. 1641. Wilton (see *D.N.B.*).
Rumper, first Protectorate Parliament. d. 1655.
Son and heir of Henry and Margaret Twysden. Many Court offices prior
to 1640 and lands worth £3000 p.a.[2]

VANE, SIR HENRY, JR. 1640. Hull (see *D.N.B.*).
Fled to Army (Percival), Rumper.
Son and heir of Sir Henry (above), Hadlow, Kent. Income at least
£7000.[3] Educated at Westminster School under Lambert Osbaldeston,
and Magdalen Hall, Oxford. Although absent during Pride's Purge
and King's trial, zealously helped the Republic, being on every committee of importance. Prior to 1640 had been in New England.
Mystic and experientialist of sorts.[4] Wife a Congregationalist, 1672.[5]

VENN, JOHN. 1641. London (see *D.N.B.*).
Survived Purge, Regicide, war service. d. 1650.
Son of Simon, St Lawrence, Somerset. Old yeoman stock. Massa-
chusetts Bay Company. Rich wool merchant. Radical, and exempted
from pardon, 1640.
Member of Christopher Love's congregation, St Anne's, Aldgate. Strong
Puritan.

VINER, SIR THOMAS (see *D.N.B.*).
Goldsmith and alderman of London. Very rich. Mayor, 1653. In favour
with Charles I, Cromwell and Charles II.
Richard Dyer, brother of a leading Independent, was his chaplain.[6]

WALLER, SIR HARDRESS. 1654. Limerick (see *D.N.B.*).
Helped in Pride's Purge, Regicide, both Protectorate Parliaments, war
service.
Son and heir of George, Groomsbridge, Kent. Professional soldier.
Irish estates. Knighted 1631.
Religious Independent.[7]

---

[1] M. F. Keeler, *op. cit.*
[2] *Ibid.*   [3] *Ibid.*
[4] Baxter, *Reliquae Baxterianae*, I, 74–6.
[5] G. Lyon-Turner, *op. cit.* II, 1002.
[6] *C.R.*   [7] Woodhouse, *op. cit.* p. 137.

Appendix A

WALLOP, ROBERT. 1640. Andover (see *D.N.B.*).

King's judge but refused to sign death warrant, Rumper, both Protectorate Parliaments.

Son and heir of Sir Henry, Farleigh Wallop, Hants, one of the wealthiest commoners of the time with manors in Hants, Wilts, Devon, Somerset, Shropshire, and lands in Ireland; gained £10,000 of Royalist lands.[1] Republican and a friend of Vane. d. m. Heveningham (q.v.). On Committee of Both Kingdoms.[2] Hart Hall, Oxford.

WALSINGHAM, SIR THOMAS. 1640. Rochester.

Rumper.

Son and heir of Sir Thomas, Chislehurst, Kent; courtier. King's, Cambridge. Probably wealthy, inheriting six manors, etc., from his father. m. (i) d. of Sir Peter Manwood; (ii) widow of Nathaniel Master, wealthy London merchant.[3]

Puritan.[4]

WALTON, VALENTINE. 1640. Hunts (see *D.N.B.*).

Regicide, Rumper, war service.

Son of Sir George, Great Stoughton, Hunts. Lands worth £400 p.a.[5] m. sister of Cromwell.[6] Genuine Republican.

Made King's Lynn, where he was Governor in 1643, a centre of Independency.[7]

WASTELL, JOHN. 1641. Northallerton.

Rumper, first Protectorate Parliament, war service.

Son and heir of Leonard, Scorton, Yorks. Sidney Sussex, Cambridge and Gray's Inn. Recorder of Richmond. Inherited probably little wealth, but became richer.[8]

WAYTE, THOMAS. 1646. Rutland (see *D.N.B.*).

Regicide, Rumper, war Service.

Son and heir of Henry, Wyndham, Leicester. Gray's Inn. Gained much royalist land—Hambleton Manor 2244 acres. Raised rents and enclosed land.[9]

---

[1] Brunton and Pennington, *op. cit.* pp. 47–8.

[2] M. F. Keeler, *op. cit.* and G. N. Godwin, *The Civil War in Hampshire*, p. 371.

[3] M. F. Keeler, *op. cit.*   [4] *Ibid.*

[5] *Ibid.*   [6] *Ibid.*

[7] Walker, *op. cit.* I, 148.   [8] M. F. Keeler, *op. cit.*

[9] *V.C.H. Rutland*, I, 198; II, 67.

WEAVER, JOHN. 1645. Stamford (see *D.N.B.*).

Fled to Army, Rumper, first Protectorate Parliament, excluded from second.

North Luppenham, Lincoln. Judge Advocate of Manchester's Army.

One of the 'godly gang'.[1] Nonconformist John Richardson preached in his house, 1672.[2] Fifth Monarchist?[3]

WENTWORTH, SIR PETER. 1640. Tamworth (see *D.N.B.*).

Refused to be King's judge, Rumper.

Son and heir of Nicholas, Lillingstone Lovell, Bucks. Probably wealthy though said he was in debt.[4] Magdalen Hall, Oxford and Lincoln's Inn. Sheriff of Oxford. Friend of Marten and Milton.

Fifth Monarchist?

WEST, EDMUND. 1641. Bucks.

Purged, entered dissent 14 May 1649, Rumper.

Marmsworth, Bucks. Brasenose, Oxford and Inner Temple. Little activity.

WESTON, BENJAMIN. 1641. Dover.

Fled to Army, refused to be King's judge, Rumper.

Fourth son of 1st Earl of Portland. m. Countess of Anglesey and gained Ashley Park Manor, Walton-on-Thames and £4000 pension arrears from Parliament for his wife.[5] Pro-Strafford (Rushworth).[6]

Presbyterian elder.[7]

WESTON, HENRY. 1646. Guildford.

Purged, Rumper?

Son of Rev. Edward, Ockham, Surrey. St John's, Oxford and Gray's Inn. Little activity.

Presbyterian elder.[8] Appointed T. Draper, on Cromwell's recommendation, to Speldhurst Church, Kent.[9]

WESTROW, THOMAS. 1646. Hythe.

Rumper.

Son of London alderman. Queen's, Oxford and Inner Temple. m.d. of Sir Henry Capell.[10] Bishops' land.

Independent.[11] Fifth monarchist?[12]

---

[1] Walker, *op. cit.* I, 95, 108, 124, 127.   [2] *C.R.*

[3] *Thurloe State Papers*, 6 Feb. 1655–6.   [4] M. F. Keeler, *op. cit.*

[5] For Weston see M. F. Keeler, *op. cit.*; *V.C.H. Surrey*, III, 73; and F. W. Brayley, *History of Surrey*, II, 105.

[6] Rushworth, *op. cit.* part III, vol. I, p. 248.

[7] Shaw, *op. cit.* II, 435.   [8] *Ibid.* p. 434.

[9] *Letters and Speeches*, 16 Nov. 1653, and *C.R.*

[10] C. V. Wedgwood's Notes.

[11] *Cal. S.P. Dom.* 1648/9, p. 334 contains an odd letter which suggests that Westrow was an Independent.

[12] *Clarendon State Papers*, in *English Hist. Rev.* (1893), p. 529.

Appendix A

WHALLEY, EDWARD (see *D.N.B.*).
Regicide, both Protectorate Parliaments.
Second son of Richard, Kirton and Screveton, Notts, and Frances, d. of Sir Henry Cromwell. Emmanuel, Cambridge. Woollen draper of Shadwell, Essex. Leader in New Model Army.
Conservative Independent.[1]   Fled to Massachusetts, 1660.

WHARTON, LORD PHILIP (see *D.N.B.*).
Fled to Army (Percival), Purged.
Second son and heir of Sir Thomas, Easby, Yorks. Grandson of 3rd Baron, and through his mother, of the Earl of Monmouth. Succeeded grandfather as 4th Lord Wharton. Estates in Yorks, Bucks, Cumberland and Westmorland. Worth £8000 p.a. m. (i) d. of Sir Rowland Wandesford, Attorney-General of Court of Wards; (ii) d. of Arthur Goodwin, acquiring manors of Winchendon, Bucks, and Woodburn, near Cookham; (iii) widow of Edward Popham.
At first wanted accommodation, then became strong supporter of Army until Pride's Purge. Friend of Cromwell. Refused to take public part in government.[2]
Leading nonconformist. In close touch with Independent ministers, one of whom, Thomas Elford, was tutor to his sons.[3]

WHITACRE, LAWRENCE. 1640. Okehampton.
Fled to Army, Rumper.
St John's, Cambridge and Middle Temple. Clerk of Privy Council, secretary to Sir Edward Philips, Master of the Rolls and soap monopolist, but sided with Parliament. Probably not very wealthy—less than £500 p.a.[4]

WHITE, WILLIAM. 1645. Pontefract.
Fled to Army (Percival), Rumper, war service.
Secretary to Fairfax. Bishops' land.

WHITELOCKE, BULSTRODE. 1640. Marlow (see *D.N.B.*).
Absent during Purge, refused to be King's judge, Rumper, both Protectorate Parliaments.
Son and heir of Sir James, Fawley Court, Bucks. St John's, Oxford and Middle Temple. m.d. of Thomas Bennett, alderman of London.

[1] *Congregational Hist. Soc. Trans.* IX, 21; Burton, *op. cit.* I, 101, 153, 260; and Firth and Davies, *Regimental History of Cromwell's Army*, p. 59.
[2] E. R. Wharton, *The Whartons of Wharton Hall*.
[3] *C.R.* under James Bedford, Thomas Benlows, Thomas Elford, etc., see index.
[4] M. F. Keeler, *op. cit.*

Almost certainly wealthy.[1] Conservative Independent, but high legal posts under Commonwealth and Protectorate. Claimed that he never let it seem that he belonged to any particular party (*Memorials*). Erastian.[2] Independent member of Cockayn's congregation.[3]

WIDDRINGTON, SIR THOMAS. 1640. Berwick (see *D.N.B.*).
Fled to Army (Percival), absent during Purge, refused to be King's judge, Rumper, both Protectorate Parliaments.
Son and heir of Lewis, Stanfordham, Northumberland. Well-known county family. A man of substance.[4] Christ Church, Oxford and Gray's Inn. m.d. of Baron Fairfax. Recorder of Berwick. Serjeant of law for Commonwealth. 'A good lawyer, but naturally a cautious and timid man'. Bishops' land.

WILDE, JOHN. 1640. Worcestershire (see *D.N.B.*).
Refused to be King's judge, Rumper.
Son and heir of George, Kempsey, Worcester. Balliol, Oxford and Inner Temple. Recorder of Worcester, 1645. m.d. and co-heir of Sir Thomas Harris, Tonge Castle, Shropshire,[5] and held much town property in Worcester.[6] On circuit, 1646. On many legal committees in Parliament.
Lay member of Westminster Assembly.

WILSON, ROWLAND. 1646. Calne (see *D.N.B.*).
Fled to Army? (Lords' Journal), refused to be King's judge, Rumper, war service, d. 1650.
Son and heir of Rowland, rich London merchant. Heir to estate of £2000 p.a.[7] Sheriff of London, July 1649. 'Very rich and vast influence in the City.'[8] Independent party.[9]
Independent. Cockayn's congregation.[10] Strong Puritan.[11]

WOGAN, THOMAS. 1646. Cardigan (see *D.N.B.*).
Fled to Army,[12] King's judge but refused to sign death warrant, Rumper, war service.
Son of John, Wiston, Pembroke, a member of the Long Parliament.

[1] M. F. Keeler, *op. cit.*   [2] Whitelocke, *Memorials*, I, 293, 503.
[3] *Congregational Hist. Soc. Trans.* (1933–5), p. 225.
[4] M. F. Keeler, *op. cit.*
[5] W. R. Williams, *Members for Worcester*, p. 42.
[6] M. F. Keeler, *op. cit.*   [7] Whitelocke, *op. cit.* § 76.
[8] Noble, *op. cit.*   [9] Whitelocke, *op. cit.* § 76.
[10] *Congregational Hist. Soc. Trans.* (1933–5), p. 225.
[11] Whitelocke, *op. cit.* § 76.
[12] This is the mythical Francis Ougaine on Rushworth's list. See *Lords' Journal*, IX, 385.

Appendix A

WOODHOUSE, SIR THOMAS. 1640. Thetford.

Rumper.

Son and heir of Sir Philip, Kimberley Hall, Norfolk. Caius, Cambridge and Lincoln's Inn. Baronet, 1623. Sheriff of Norfolk, 1624-5. m.d. of Baron Hunsdon. Gentleman of the chamber to Henry, Prince of Wales. Estate worth £2000.[1]

Strongly Calvinistic.[2]

WROTHE, SIR THOMAS. 1645. Bridgwater.

Survived Purge, King's judge but refused to sign death warrant, second Protectorate Parliament.

Son and heir of Thomas, North Pedderton, near Bridgwater, Somerset, and Newton Manor. Gloucester Hall, Oxford and Inner Temple. m.d. of Nathaniel Rich. Sheriff of Somerset[3] 1639-40. Colonizing activity. 1620, Council for New England. Moved impeachment of Charles.[4]

Presbyterian elder.[5] Radical Puritan.[6]

The following members of Parliament, added for the sake of completeness, are listed by Brunton and Pennington as having survived Pride's Purge. I know nothing of their religious affiliations.

Edward Apsley (Steyning). Son and heir of Sir Edward of Speckham, Sussex.

Francis Bacon (Ipswich). Fifth son of Sir Nicholas; Ipswich town council.

John Barker (Coventry). Merchant and mayor of Coventry, 1634.

William Carent (Milborne Port).

Richard Edwards (Christchurch). Son and heir of Richard, Artesy, Bedford.

Samuel Gardiner (Evesham). Mayor of Evesham.

John Herbert (Monmouthshire). Youngest son of Philip, Earl of Pembroke.

Thomas Hussey (Whitchurch).

John Lowry (Cambridge).

Sir Richard Lucy (Old Sarum).

Christopher Martyn (Plympton Earl).

[1] Bloomfield, *Norfolk*, II, 555, and M. F. Keeler, *op. cit.*

[2] M. F. Keeler, *op. cit.* quotes his letter regretting the growth of the 'sublapsarions', i.e. those who held a less rigorous doctrine of Predestination.

[3] Collinson, *History of Somerset*, III, 62-80.

[4] S. R. Gardiner, *History of the Great Civil War*, IV, 50.

[5] Shaw, *op. cit.* II, 421.

[6] *Cal. S.P. Dom.* (1635), p. 377.

Sir Roger North (Eye).
Richard Norton (Hampshire).
Francis Pierpont (Nottingham).
Carew Raleigh (Haslemere).
Francis Russell (Cambridgeshire). Fled to the Army 1647 (Percival).
John Stephens (Tewkesbury). Fled to the Army 1647 (Percival).
George Wylde (Droitwich).

STATISTICAL ANALYSIS OF TABLE A

In the table (opposite):

The religious categories should not be regarded as watertight divisions.

Those marked as 'Independents' were certainly so.

Those marked as 'Probable Independents' are those for whom there is only some testimony to support the statement, or non-conclusive evidence with nothing to the contrary.

Those marked 'non-Puritan' include such men as Marten, who were not members of Independent congregations, yet wanted toleration.

Those marked as 'Sectaries' are all known to belong to a radical non-Independent religious group. When other evidence is lacking, Fifth Monarchists have been included in this group.

Those marked as 'Puritans' are certainly Puritan, but there is no evidence regarding their denominational affiliation.

Those marked as 'Possible Presbyterians' are those about whom the only evidence is that at one time they were Presbyterian. It is quite likely, however, that they, too, became Independents, as so many other 'Presbyterians' did.

Those marked as 'Uncertain' are those for whom there is no evidence of religious attitudes. It is, however, almost certain that such a one as Thomas Pride was an Independent or a sectary.

The sociological groupings are anything but satisfactory, due to difficulties of definition as well as lack of material. Should a leading gentleman and county official from a poor county in North England, very poor by comparison with similar men in wealthy counties, be nevertheless classed as a greater gentleman? He is, in terms of social influence and clientele. He is not, in terms of wealth. Similarly, would the younger son of a peer have a greater social influence than the eldest son of a wealthy gentleman?

STATISTICAL ANALYSIS OF APPENDIX A

	Political Activity											Religion						
	Total	Fled to Army	Probably purged	Refused to be King's Judge	King's judge but refused to sign death warrant	Regicide	Rumper	Saints' Parliament	First Protectorate Parliament	Second Protectorate Parliament	Second Protectorate Parliament excluded	Independent	Probably Independent	Non-Puritan, pro-toleration	Sectary	Uncertain but Puritan	Uncertain, possibly Presbyterian	Unknown
Fled to Army 1647[1]	74		8	20	9	19	65	6	23	12	8	18	15	1	6	14	4	16
Probably purged[2]	23	8					13	1	7	7	1	6	5		1	5	1	5
Refused to be King's Judge	49	20					46	3	21	12	7	11	11		3	10	4	10
King's judge but refused to sign death warrant[3]	21	9					19			4		5	1	1	1	5		8
Regicide[4]	59	19					40	5	15	12	2	21	3	1	9	8	1	16
Rumper[5]	193	65	13	46	19	40		18	64	39	16	36	29	4	13	34	12	65
Saints' Parliament[6]	22	6	1	3		5	18		14	14		5	5		8	2	1	1
First Protectorate Parliament[7]	78	23	7	21		15	64	14		42		23	17	1	9	12	3	13
Second Protectorate Parliament[8]	52	12	7	12	4	12	39	14	42			18	10		4	10	2	8
Second Protectorate Parliament excluded	20	8	1	7		2	16					5	5		2	4	1	3
Greater gentry	52	26	8	14	5	7	48	4	20	13	4	13	5	1	3	16	3	11
Gentry	53	21	7	11	6	15	47	5	17	14	5	8	10	1	5	10	2	17
Lesser and declining gentry	37	12	5	8	2	11	33	3	11	5	6	12	7	1	2	3	2	10
London merchants	23	2	1	4	3	7	10	4	5	3	2	10	3	1	5	3		1
Country merchants	19	4		4	2	5	18	4	6	5		1	3		1	4	1	9
Lawyers	37	7	2	8	2	8	32	1	16	9	3	7	7	1	4	3	3	12
Unclassified	12	2			1	6	5	1	3	3		3	1		1			7
Totals												54	36	5	21	39	11	69

[1] A conflation of names from all sources. The actual number was fifty-eight. See above, p. 69.

[2] All names on any purge-list included. It does not prove they were purged, but it would suggest that they were not obvious Independents at the time of Pride's Purge.

[3] Sat in the court that tried the King, but did not sign the death warrant.

[4] Actually signed the death warrant.

[5] From H. A. Glass, *The Barebones Parliament.*

[6] According to Brunton and Pennington, *op. cit.*

[7] Mainly from lists in Cobbett, *Parliamentary History,* III.

[8] Whitelocke, *Memorials,* IV, 280.

An arbitrary kind of ruling has been made where there is no certain knowledge of status. Those with incomes above £2000 p.a. (excluding, of course, gains after 1642), peers and sons of peers (except where the latter were notoriously poor), and those who apparently held positions of social importance in their counties, are all included as 'Greater gentry'. So in East Anglia, the Mashams and Barringtons are classified as greater gentry; the Brewsters as lesser.

Those marked as 'Lesser gentry' are those whose incomes are known to have been less than £2000 p.a. and those who were declining, for example, Sir John Danvers.

For slightly more than half the list, however, there is still insufficient evidence to justify either category, and these have been grouped as 'Gentry'. In view of the lack of evidence as to status, it is possible, but not proven, that most were, in fact, lesser gentry.

Again, through lack of evidence in all cases, no differentiation has been made between greater and lesser merchants, or important and minor lawyers.

Even from these very uncertain figures, a few facts do emerge. A larger percentage of the lesser gentry than of the greater were Regicides, but a larger percentage of the greater gentry fled to the Army in 1647. Percentages of those taking part in the Rump were roughly even, and also of those who were probably excluded at Pride's Purge. The percentage of certain or probable Independents and sectaries is slightly higher among the London merchants and lesser gentry (although in the former group a few names were added to the list simply because they were known to be religious Independents). However, the number of probable omissions makes any generalizing on social and religious inter-relationships dangerous, and the only value of the analysis in this regard is to show that at least there was a fairly consistent percentage of religious Independents among all the social groupings in the party.

APPENDIX B

A contemporary list of radical members at the time of Pride's Purge

THE following list is from a little-known but important pamphlet published a few days after Pride's Purge, giving a list of those regarded by its author(s) as the real radicals of Parliament. It appears to be reasonably accurate, as it omits the more conservative Independents, such as Armine and those known to have been absent at the time, such as St John, Whitelocke, Vane, etc.

A Remonstrance and Declaration of several Counties, Cities and Boroughs against the Unfaithfulness and late unwarrantable Proceedings of Some of their Knights, Citizens and Burgesses in Parliament.[1]

We the knights etc. neither gave nor intended to give to

Henry Marten	Thomas Harrison	Wm. Lenthall (Speaker)
Henry Smith	Francis Rous	Lord William Monson
John Hutchinson	Gregory Clement	Philip Lord Lisle
Humphrey Edwards	Augustine Skinner	Robert Blake
Humphrey Salway	Sir Gilbert Pickering	William Cowley
Thomas Purey	Sir James Harrington	Henry Ireton
Isaac Pennington	Edmund Ludlow	Sir Edward Bainton
John Lisle	William Edwards[3]	Philip Smith
Michael Oldsworth	Nicholas Love	Peregrine Pelham
Thomas Scott	Thomas Atkins	Thomas Challoner
Edmund Dunch	Luke Hodges	Brian Stapleton
Nicholas Gold	Sir William Allanson	William Hay
Valentine Walton	Cornelius Holland	Oliver Cromwell
Henry Herbert	John Carew	Denis Bond
Thomas Waite	Benjamin Valentine	John Fry
Anthony Stapley	Francis Allen	Sir Michael Livesey
John Jones	Lawrence Whitacre	Peter Temple
John Lenthall	Roger Hill	Miles Corbet
John Venn	Sir Henry Mildmay	George Thomson
Richard Aldworth	Thomas Lord Grey	Sir Peter Wentworth
John Dure[2]	John Moore	John Gurdon

[1] B.M., E 536, vol. 402. [2] John Dove?
[3] Richard Edwards?

Sir Thomas Wrothe	Philip Skippon	Gregory Norton
James Temple	Edmund Prideaux	John Downes
Richard Salway	John Trenchard	Rowland Wilson
Sir John Danvers	Augustine Garland	Edmund Harvey
William Purefoy	Alexander Rigby	Godfrey Bosville
William Constable	John Blackeston	Sir John Bourchier
Francis Thorpe	George Snelling	Thomas Malevors
James Challoner	John Corbet	William White
Thomas Westrow	George Serle	Algernon Sidney

the right to depose or execute the King, disinherit his children, to break the personal treaty with the King [re Peace] nor to reject the King's promises of future security or the altering of the government by Kings, Lords and Commons, or tolerating of all kinds of Religious Heresies and Errors, the taking away of our Ministers tithes and useful Maintenance, or the disorderly intruding into their sacred Function without any calling or Ordination thereunto, nor especially to break the liberties of Parliament.

This is the most radical list that has come to hand, including as it does the most radical members of the Independent party at the time of Pride's Purge. It is interesting, then, to notice that they were not all consistently radical throughout. Of these eighty-nine, forty had fled to the Army in 1647; twenty refused to take part in the King's trial; twelve did, but refused to sign the death warrant; thirty-three were actual Regicides; seventy-eight were Rumpers; eight sat in the Saints' Parliament; thirty-two in the First Protectorate Parliament; twenty in the Second, plus five excluded from it.

Fifteen were certainly religious Independents, fifteen probably so, two non-Puritans favouring toleration, ten sectaries, nine unidentified Puritans, six possibly Presbyterians, and thirty-five unknown.

APPENDIX C

Congregational Ministers, 1640–60

THE following is a list of all the Congregationalist ministers (including those of doubtful authenticity) in England between 1640 and 1660 that I have been able to discover. About 200 were certainly Congregationalists and were listed as such by Calamy, who for apologetic reasons did not emphasize the divisions in the nonconformist ranks, and so presumably did not always note the fact that they were Independents. Those listed by Calamy as Congregationalists are almost certainly such; their names are printed in italic.

The remainder are probably or possibly Congregationalists. They include all those who applied for licences to preach as Independents in 1672, those who were in New England and returned after the outbreak of the Civil War, those who appeared as strong supporters of the Commonwealth and Protectorate governments, or were favoured by them, and those who were close associates or relations of other Independent ministers, when there is no contrary evidence that they were Presbyterians or sectaries.

Most of the names and information are in *Calamy Revised*, which is the source when no other reference is given.

The ministers are listed by counties. Where one minister moved from one county to another, he is listed in both, and an asterisk indicates that the name appears in more than one place. Ministers with the same name are differentiated by roman numerals. Where the patrons are known, their names are in brackets after the name of the parish. 'Holland' or 'New England' given in brackets at the end of the entry indicates that the minister emigrated, but returned to England after the outbreak of the Civil War.

This appendix may help in the further identification of Independent members of Parliament and religious Independency. Some odd factors have already emerged. In Kent and Yorkshire, although both counties could show many Independent members and ministers, I have been able to find practically no definite connexions between the two groups; and in East Anglia, although there were a great number of Independent ministers, indicating substantial support, there are fewer Independent members of Parliament than one might expect.

BEDFORDSHIRE

*Corbyn, Samuel   Shillington, 1654
Dell, William   Chaplain to Fairfax, 1643; Yelden, 1640
Donne, John   Pertenhall, 1653
*Eston, John   Pertenhall
Fairclough, Samuel   Houghton Conquest, 1655
*Geare, Allan   Woburn, 1656
*Negus, Strickland   Melchbourne, 1645
*Poynter, John   Houghton Conquest, 1654 (Cromwell)
Wheeler, William   Cranfield

BERKSHIRE

Batchelor, John   Windsor Castle, 1650
*Biscoe, John   Abingdon, 1657
Gilbert, Thomas (I)   St Lawrence, Reading, 1648
Mayne, Zachary   Lecturer at Abingdon, 1657
Woodward, Hezekiah   Bray, 1650

BUCKINGHAMSHIRE

Batchelor, John   Datchet, 1659
Dyer, William   Cholesbury; (later Quaker)
Fownes, George   High Wycombe, 1657; (later Baptist)
Gibbs, John   Newport Pagnell, 1652
*Gilbert, Thomas (I)   Upper Wichendon (Lord Wharton)
Hall, Robert   Colnbrook, 1651
Lockyer, Nicholas   Farnham Royal, 1650
*Maidwell, John   Simpson, 1647
*Mead, Matthew   Preacher to Council at Whitehall; Great Brickhill, 1654
*Terry, Edward   Amersham, 1657
Valentine, Thomas   Chalfont St Giles, 1625; (friend of Fleetwood)
Wilson, John (I)   Aylesbury School, 1655; Hulcott, 1657; chaplain to Sir Richard Ingoldsby

CAMBRIDGESHIRE

*Erbury, William[1]   Chaplain in Skippon's regiment; lecturer around Ely
Fido, John   Hardwick, 1649
Holcroft, Francis   Bassingbourn, 1655

[1] *D.N.B.*

Appendix C

*Nye, John   Cottenham, 1654
*Sedgwick, William   Ely, 1645
Sheldrake, *William*   Leverington, 1654 (Thurloe); Elm, 1657 (Thurloe);
   lecturer at Wisbech, 1655

CHESHIRE

Eaton, *Samuel*   Congregational church at Dukinfield, 1644–58
*Gilbert, Thomas (I)   Cheadle
Harrison, *Thomas*   St Oswald's, Chester, 1661
*Machin, John   Whitley, Great Budworth, 1661
Moxon, *George* (I)   Newbold Astbury, 1654; (emigrated to New England)
*Shawe, John   Lymm, 1643
*Smallwood, Thomas   Thurstaston, 1638; Nether Peover, 1639
Wilson, John (II)

CORNWALL

Hull, *Joseph*   Launceston, 1648; St Buryan, 1656; (emigrated to New
   England, 1635)
*Mall, Thomas   Fowey, 1653
*Morton, Charles   Blisland, 1656
Peters, Thomas[1]   Mylor
*Powel, Thomas   Truro, 1557
*Tookey, Job   St Ives, 1643

CUMBERLAND

Atkinson, *Simon*   Crosthwaite, 1645; Lazonby, 1660
Benson, *George*   Bridekirk, 1649
*Davis, John   Hutton and Castle Sowerby, 1651; Kirkoswald, 1655
*Gilpin, Richard   Greystoke, 1652
Hopkins, *William*   Kirkoswald, 1651; Melmerby, 1655
*Lampit, William   Ejected from Aikton by Haselrig, 1650; (unorthodox)
Larkham, *George*   Embleton, Brigham; and Cockermouth, 1651
*Marsden, Jeremiah   Edenhall, 1658
Nicholson, *George*   Melmerby
*Polwhele, Theophilus   Carlisle, 1651
*Starr, Comfort   Carlisle, 1656; (New England)

DERBYSHIRE

Ford, *Thomas*   Chesterfield, 1656
*Machin, John   Lecturer at Ashbourne
*Palmer, Thomas   Aston-on-Trent, 1646

---

[1] W. L. Sachse, 'The Migration of New Englanders to America', *American Historical Review*, LIII, 264.

DEVONSHIRE

Ashwood, Bartholomew   Bickleigh, 1650; Axminster, 1656
Bartlet, John   Fremington, 1656
Bartlet, William   Bideford, 1651; (Separatist group, 1658)
Birdwood, James   Dartmouth, 1658
Bullhead, John[1]   Ashreigney
Chishul, John   Tiverton, Pitt Portion, 1654
Coven, Stephen   Sampford Peverell, 1655
Flavell, John   Lecturer at St Saviour's, Dartmouth, 1656
Geare, Allan   Dartmouth, 1656
Hughes, George   St Andrew's, Plymouth, 1643
Larkham, Thomas   Tavistock, 1648; (New England)
Mall, Thomas[2]   Preacher at Exeter Cathedral, 1655
Martyn, Thomas   St Andrew's, Plymouth, 1650
Mather, Increase   Great Torrington, 1658; chaplain to Colonel Bingham 1659
Mather, Nathaniel   Harberton, 1656; Barnstaple, 1657; (educated in New England)
Peard, Oliver   Barnstaple
Polwhele, Theophilus   Tiverton, 1655
Powel, Thomas   Exeter, 1658
Rowe, John   Tiverton, 1654
Stucley, Lewis[2]   Newtown Ferrers and Great Torrington, 1646; Tiverton, 1651; Exeter Cathedral, 1656
Tucker, Edmund   Dittisham, 1654; Halwell
Wellman, Thomas   Luppitt, 1640

DORSET

Alleine, William   Blandford Forum, 1646
Backaller, Henry   Wambrook, 1646
Bampfield, Francis   Wraxall (John Bampfield), 1646; Sherborne, 1657
Bartlet, Robert   Over Compton, 1656
Benn, William   All Hallows, Dorchester, 1629
Brice, John   West Chickerell, 1659
Butler, Henry   Dorchester, 1651–6; (educated in New England)
Chauncey, Ichabod   Compton, 1657; (educated in New England)
Churchill, Joshua   Over Compton, 1650; Winterborne Came, 1655; Fordington, 1656

---

[1] On a list of Congregational ministers petitioning Charles II, P.R.O.; S.P. 29-1-28.
[2] W. J. Harte, *Devonshire Association Transactions* (1937), pp. 44 ff.

Crane, Thomas[1] Rampisham, 1658 (Cromwell)

Damer, Edward Chaplain to Guernsey garrison, 1656; Wyke Regis, 1658

Down, Richard Winterborne Monkton, 1658

Eaton, John Cerne Abbas, 1648; Bridport, 1649

Lamb, Philip Alton Pancras, 1648; Bere Regis, 1655

Light, John Preston with Sutton Points, 1657

Loder, John Fordington, 1648

Polwhele, Theophilus Langton Long, Blandford, 1649

Thorne, George Weymouth, 1648; Melcombe Regis, 1654; Melcombe and Radipole, 1656

Westley, John Chaplain on board the *Triumph*, 1657; Winterborne Whitchurch, 1658

DURHAM

Gilpin, Richard Durham Cathedral, 1649

Hammond, Samuel Bishopwearmouth, 1651; appointed lecturer at St Nicholas', Newcastle, by Corporation, 1652; and to St Magdalen's Hospital and St Thomas' Chapel by Haselrig; activity on behalf of government

Ward, Ralph Wolsingham, 1653

Weld, Thomas Gateshead, 1650; (friend of Hugh Peters; New England)

Williamson, Edward Washington, 1655 (Cromwell)

ESSEX

Amyraut, Paul East Dereham, 1648; Wanstead, 1654; (Holland)

Bulkley, John Fordham, 1650; (educated in New England)

Clark, Thomas Stisted; 1647

Cockayn, George All Hallows, Barking, 1642

Collier, Abel West Takeley, 1654

Farnworth, Joseph South Hanningfield, 1655 (Hugh Peters); (New England)

Firmin, Giles Shalford, 1648; (New England)

Gouge, Robert Maldon, Ipswich, 1655

Hoar, Leonard Wanstead, 1656, (educated in New England)

Holbeck, Martin High Easter, 1649

Lawson, Thomas Langenhoe, 1645; Fingringhoe, 1646

Lowry, Thomas Great Braxted, 1642

Lucas, John Ugley, 1649?

---

[1] W. Densham and J. Ogle, *The Story of Congregational Churches in Dorset*, p. 6.

Lukin, Henry   Chipping Ongar, 1658; later chaplain to Sir William Masham
Malbon, Samuel   Henham, 1654; (educated in New England)
Morton, Charles   Takeley, 1653
Moxon, George (II)   Radwinter, 1660
Owen, John   Fordham, 1643; Coggeshall, 1646
Robotham, John   Upminster, 1656
Sams, John   Kelvedon, 1647; Coggeshall, 1652; (New England)
Sedgwick, Obadiah[1]   Coggeshall, 1639 (Earl of Warwick)
Sedgwick, William[1]   Farnham, 1635–44
Sparrow, William   Halstead, 1650
Stalham, John   Terling, 1632
*Stileman, Samuel   West Hanningfield, 1650
*Storer, John   Barking, 1647
Tuke, Lemuel   Rayne, 1642, Steeple
Warren, John   Hatfield Broad Oak, 1646
Waterhouse, Thomas   Ash Bocking, 1652; Little Hallingbury, 1658; (New England)
*Wilson, John (III)   Moreton, 1637; Little Hallingbury, 1647
Yates, John   West Ham, 1650

GLOUCESTERSHIRE
Beale, William   Stow-on-the-Wold, 1648; (political radical)
Becket, William   Buckland, 1657; Compton Abdale, 1658; (political radical)
Cooper, John   Cheltenham, 1650; (Socinian)
Davison, William   Notgrove
Dunce, John   Hazleton, 1654
Fletcher, Edward   Bagendon, 1657; (New England)
Forbes, James   Preacher at Gloucester Cathedral, 1654
Harris, Francis   Deerhurst, 1651; (political radical)
Head, Joshua   Bishop's Cleeve?
Helme, Carnsew   Winchcomb, 1654; Sudeley, 1655
Knowles, John   St Werburgh's, Bristol, 1653; (New England)
Langston, John   Ashchurch, 1660
Mather, Increase   St Mary de Load, Gloucester, 1659
Palmer, Anthony   Bourton-on-the-Water, 1646; (political radical)
Smith, Jonathan   Hempstead, 1658
Smith, Thomas (I)   Longhope, 1656
Tray, William   Oddington, 1646; (political radical)
*Troughton, William   Deerhurst, 1648
Wells, John   Tewkesbury, 1651

[1] *D.N.B.*

138

Appendix C

HAMPSHIRE

Coxe, Henry Bishopstoke, 1654

*Crofts, John Carisbrooke, Isle of Wight, 1651; Mottisfont, 1654; chaplain to Alice Lisle, wife of the Regicide, 1669

Gale, Theophilus Preacher at Winchester Cathedral, 1657

Lancaster, Robert Quarley, 1648; Amport, 1656; (Antinomian)

*Lawrence, George St Cross Hospital, Winchester, 1651

*Marshall, Walter Hursley, 1656

Martyn, John Newport, Isle of Wight, 1650; Yarmouth, Isle of Wight, 1658

Oakes, Urian Titchfield; (New England)

Robinson, Nathaniel Southampton *c.* 1646

Rogers, Robert Deane, 1646

Say, Giles Catherington, 1655; St Michael's, Southampton, 1657 (Cromwell)

Sprint, Samuel South Tidworth, 1654

*Troughton, William Chaplain to Robert Hammond, Isle of Wight, 1647

Warner, John[1] Christchurch (John Moyle)

Whitmarsh, George Rowner, 1658

HEREFORDSHIRE

Garnons, John Little Hereford, 1651

HERTFORDSHIRE

Bedford, Isaac Lecturer at Hitchin, 1642; Willian, 1645

*Cradock, Samuel Little Berkhamsted, 1645

Eeles, Nathaniel Harpenden, Wheathampstead, 1643

Haworth, William Lecturer at St Alban's

Loeffs, Isaac Shenley, 1650

*Partridge, Nathaniel St Alban's, 1657

Tookey, Job Preacher at St Alban's Abbey, 1648

*Tutty, William Totteridge, 1646; chaplain to Colonel Markham

Walley, Thomas Rickmansworth, 1645

Wilson, John (III) Kimpton, 1657

Yates, John Cheshunt, 1656

HUNTINGDONSHIRE

Luddington, Robert Kimbolton, 1643

*Negus, Strickland Yelling, 1652

Nye, Philip Kimbolton *c.* 1641

---

[1] *Congregational Hist. Soc. Trans.* IX, 31.

*Poynter, John Lecturer at Huntingdon, 1632 (Mercers' Company, London)
*Yaxley, John Stibbington, 1639

KENT

*Aires,—? Fairlawn, Shipborne; (see Lincolnshire list)
Alexander, Edward Wickhambreaux, 1652; St Margaret's, Rochester, 1659
*Batchelor, John Lecturer at Lewisham, 1642
Barton, John Egerton, 1643; Harrietsham, 1646; Bishopsbourne with Barham, 1652
*Clarkson, David Crayford, 1650
Darby, — Fairlawn, Shipborne? (Vane's house)
*Davis, John (II) Congregational Church, Dover; chaplain to Thomas Kelsey
Draper, Thomas Speldhurst, 1654 (recommended by Cromwell)
Durant, John St George's, Canterbury, 1649
*Ferguson, Robert Godmersham, 1657
*Hemmings, Joseph Lydd, 1657; chaplain to Colonel Pride
Jacob, William Wade
Lane, Richard Chislet and Northbourne, 1656
*Larkham, Thomas Greenwich, 1645; (father of George; New England)
*Malory, Thomas Deptford, 1652
*Mather, Nathaniel Sandwich, 1655; (educated in New England)
Nichols, Charles Canterbury and Adisham, 1650
*Norcross, Nathaniel Dover, 1653; (emigrated to New England)
Osborne, Joseph Brenchley, 1646; Benenden, 1658
Player, John Canterbury, 1646
*Robotham, John Dover, c. 1654
*Sams, John West Farleigh, 1645; (emigrated to New England)
Ventress, Thomas St Margaret's, Canterbury, 1654
Whiston, Joseph Maidstone, 1656; chaplain to Major-General Harrison

LANCASHIRE

Ambrose, Joshua West Derby, Walton; (emigrated to New England)
Ambrose, Nehemiah Kirkby, Walton; (emigrated to New England)
Ashley, Richard Blackrod, Bolton, 1661
Briscoe, Michael Walmsley, Bolton, 1648
Camelford, Gabriel Staveley, Cartmel, 1649
Harrison, Cuthbert Singleton, 1651
Jollie, Thomas Altham, Whalley, 1649
*Lampit, William Ulverston; (unorthodox)

Parke, *Robert* (I)   Bolton-le-Moors, 1645
Parr, John
*Town, *Robert*   Heywood, 1640; Todmorden, 1643; Elland, 1652;
   (Antinomian)
Wigan, John   Gorton, 1642; Heapey and Birch, 1644, Manchester, 1656

LEICESTERSHIRE

Clark, Matthew   Narborough (William Woolaston)
Langdale, Thomas   Great Bowden, 1659
*Lowry, Thomas   Market Harborough
*Maidwell, John   Claybrooke, 1646
Smith, Thomas (II)   Castle Donnington, 1657
*Troughton, William   Wanlip, 1650
* *Weld, Thomas*   Wanlip, 1646
*Yaxley, John   Kibworth Beauchamp, 1647

LINCOLNSHIRE

*Aires—?   Glentworth (possibly the same as James Ayers, licensed
   Congregational at the house of Lady Vane. See Kent list)
Alford, Robert   Ludborough
Anderson, Bankes   Town preacher at Boston, 1651
Cramlington, Robert   Little Carlton, 1654; Manby and Hogsthorpe, 1656
Finch, Martin   Aby and Belleau, 1654; Tetney, 1654; Humberstone, 1656
Reyner, Edward[1]   Lincoln, 1626–60
Ryther, John   Frodingham, 1655
*Tricket, Mark   Gate Burton, 1662
* *Wood, Seth*   Lavington, 1639

LONDON

Barker, Matthew   St Leonard's, Eastcheap, 1649
Bragge, Robert   All-Hallows-the-Great, 1652
Brooks, Thomas   St Margaret's, New Fish Street, 1648
Burton, Henry[2]   St Matthew's, Friday Street, 1642
Burroughs, Jeremiah[2]   Stepney; Cripplegate; (Holland)
Canne, John[2]   London
Caryl, Joseph   Preacher at Lincoln's Inn, 1632–47; Westminster Abbey,
   1649–60
Chandler, Thomas   London
*Cockayn, George   Chaplain in Fleetwood's regiment, 1651; St Pancras,
   Soper Lane, 1646

---

[1] Calamy, *Account*, p. 443.   [2] *D.N.B.*

Collins, *John*   Lecturer at St Antholin's? (educated in New England; preacher in Scotland)

Conyers, Tobias   St Ethelburga's, Bishopsgate, 1659

*Cooper, William   Lecturer, Westminster Abbey, 1654

*Craddock, Walter[1,2]   London

**Davis, John* (II)   Lecturer at Christ Church

Davy, Humphrey[1]   London

Dyer, Richard   Lecturer at St Peter's Cheap, 1646; Lord Mayor's chaplain to Sir Thomas Adams, John Kendrick, Thomas Viner

Dyer, *Samuel*   All Hallows, 1654; St Nicholas Olave, 1654

*Erbury, William[2]   Christ Church, Newgate Street

**Eyre, William*   St Michael's, Queenhithe

Feake, Christopher[3]   Broken Wharf

*Geare, Allan   St Bennet, Paul's Wharf, 1649

Goodwin, John   St Stephen's, Coleman Street, 1633

Griffiths, George   Lecturer, St Bartholomew's, Exchange, Westminster Abbey and Charterhouse

Harrison, Thomas   Chaplain to Army in Ireland; St Dunstan's-in-the-East, 1651; (New England)

Hodges, John   Tower of London, 1655

Holmes, Nathaniel   St Mary Staining, 1643

Hooke, William   Master of the Savoy, 1659; (emigrated to New England, 1637)

Juxon, Nicholas[1]   London

Kentish, Richard   Lecturer at St Katherine's-by-the-Tower, 1639

*Lawrence, George   St George's, Botolph Lane, 1640

**Lee, Samuel*   St Botolph's, Bishopsgate, 1655

**Loder, John*   St Bartholomew's, Exchange, 1656 (Cromwell)

*Maidwell, John   St Catherine's, Coleman Street, 1645

**Malory, Thomas*   Lecturer at St Michael's, Crooked Lane, 1658

Newan, Robert[1]   London

Onge, Thomas[1]   London

**Palmer, Thomas*   Chaplain in Skippon's regiment, 1644; St Lawrence Pountney, 1644

*Pearse, Edward   Lecturer at St Margaret's, Westminster, 1657; the Abbey, 1658

Roberts, Nicholas[1]   London

Rogers, John[2,3]   Trinity Lane

**Rowe, John*   Westminster Abbey, 1655

---

[1] *The Clarke Papers* (Camden Society), IV, 82.   [2] *D.N.B.*

[3] On a list of Congregational ministers in and around London *c.* 1660, P.R.O.; S.P. 29-47-75.

Appendix C

*Sedgwick, Obadiah[1] St Mildred's, 1640; St Andrew's, Holborn; St Paul's, Covent Garden

Scobell, Henry[2] London

*Simpson, Sidrach[1] St Margaret's, 1641; St Mary Abchurch, 1650; St Bartholomew's, Exchange, 1653; (Amsterdam)

*Simpson, John[3] Lecturer, St Botolph's, Aldgate; (great Antinomian)

*Slater, Samuel Lecturer, St Katherine's-by-the-Tower, 1628

*Sprigge, Joshua[1] St Mary's Aldermary and St Pancras, Soper Lane

*Sterry, Peter Cromwell's chaplain; lecturer at St Helen's, Bishopsgate

Strong, William[1, 4] St Dunstan's-in-the-West and Westminster Abbey

*Tookey, Job St Martin's Vintry, 1648

*Tutty, William St Martin Orgar, 1645

*Venning, Ralph Chaplain at Tower of London, 1648; lecturer at St Mary Magdalen, Milk Street, 1658

Viner, William[2] London

Willer, Jacob[2] London

Wise, Lawrence Garlickhithe, 1649; chaplain to Navy, 1654

*Wood, Seth Christ Church, 1654; lecturer at Westminster Abbey, 1655

MIDDLESEX

*Bartlet, William Wapping, 1647; (Separatist group, 1658)

*Byefield, Adoniram[1] Fulham, 1645

*Elford, Thomas Acton, 1656

*Gilbert, Thomas (II) Ealing, 1651

*Greenhill, William Stepney, 1652

*Knowles, John Twickenham, 1652; (emigrated to New England)

*Mead, Matthew Shadwell, Stepney, 1658

*Nye, John Acton, 1650

*Nye, Philip Acton, 1643

Roll, William Pinner, Harrow, 1650

*Terry, Edward Great Greenford, 1661

*Tutty, William South Mimms, 1642

*Valentine, Thomas St Mary's, Whitechapel, 1654

*Walley, Thomas Whitechapel, 1646

Warham, Francis Hendon, 1643

Willis, Thomas (I) Twickenham; (allegedly very opposed to Charles I; New England)

[1] D.N.B.
[2] The Clarke Papers (Camden Society), IV, 82.
[3] On a list of Congregational ministers in and around London c. 1660, P.R.O.; S.P. 29-47-75.
[4] Ira Brosely, Ministers of the Abbey Church.

143

The Independents in the Civil War

MONMOUTHSHIRE

*Craddock, Walter[1, 2]   Monmouth
*Gilbert, Thomas (II)   Nash, 1635 (Lord Wharton); (Ireland?)
Wroth, William[1]   Llonvaches (d. 1642)

NORFOLK

Alexander, Samuel   Godwick, 1652; Stanfield, 1654 (Sir Thomas L'Estrange)
Allen, John   Yarmouth, 1650
Allen, Thomas   City preacher of Norwich, St George's, Tombland,
    Norwich, 1657; (fled to Holland, 1636; New England, 1638)
Amyraut, Christopher   Hindringham, 1652; New Buckenham, 1657
*Amyraut, Paul   Mundesley; (Holland)
Armitage, Timothy[3]   Norwich
Benton, Thomas (I)   Pulham Market, 1654; Pulham St Mary, 1657
Benton, Thomas (II)   Stratton St Michael, 1657
Breviter, Richard   North Walsham, 1651; (Separatist, 1656)
Brewster, N.[3]   Alby
Bridbank, William[3]   Tunstead and Scottow, 1656
Bridge, William   Town preacher, Yarmouth, 1642; pastor of Norwich
    Congregational Church, 1642
Cocke, Robert[3]   Yarmouth
Cory, John   Happisburgh and Walcott, 1656
Crushing, Peter[3]   Yarmouth and Lessingham
Green, John   Tunstead, 1657
Horne, John   All Hallows, South Lynn, 1643
Lawrence, Richard   Walsingham, 1651; Stratton St Michael, 1654; Bran-
    caster, 1655; Trunch with Swafield, 1655
*Lawson, Thomas   Norwich, 1649; Denton, 1655; Market Weston
Leverington, John   Neatishead with Irstead
Lougher, John   Letheringsett, 1655; Baconsthorpe, 1661
*Lucas, John   Stalham, 1658; Ingham, 1659
*Malbon, Samuel   Blofield, 1660; (educated in New England)
Martyn, John[3]   Edgefield, 1653
Money, John   Wymondham, 1642
Newman, Thomas   Heydon, 1652
*Norcross, Nathaniel   Little Walsingham, 1655; Waterden, 1658
*Oxenbridge, John   Yarmouth, 1643
Purt, Robert   Garvestone with Whinburgh, 1654
Reyner, John   Happisburgh, 1650; Rollesby, 1656

---

[1] D.N.B.   [2] Congregational Hist. Soc. Trans. XIII, 13.
[3] J. Browne, History of Congregationalism in Norfolk and Suffolk.

*Sumptner, Charles   Runcton Holme, 1658
Taylor, Thomas   Godwick, 1653
*Tillinghast, John[1]   Trunch
Tookey, Job   Yarmouth, 1652
*Wale,—[2]   Hapton
Woodward, Enoch   Catton, 1658
Worts, Richard   Guestwick, 1650; Foulsham with Themelthorpe, 1654
Worts, Thomas   Banningham, 1656 (Cromwell)

NORTHAMPTONSHIRE

Browning, Thomas   Desborough, 1657
Clark, Matthew   Chaplain to Colonel Francis Hacker, Ashley, 1655
Courtman, John   Irchester, 1653; Thorpe Malsor, 1654 (John Mansell)
Floyde, William   Woodford, 1645
Gunter, John   Whittlebury; Cromwell's chaplain
*Maidwell, John   Kettering, 1651
*Negus, Strickland   Irchester
Resbury, Richard   Oundle, 1641
Whiting, Nathaniel   Lowick, 1648; Aldwinkle All Saints, 1653
*Wright, James   Green's Norton, 1646
*Yaxley, John   Thornaugh, 1642

NORTHUMBERLAND

Benlows, Thomas   Mitford, 1652
Davis, John (I)   Bywell St Peter, 1658
Durant, William   Various churches at Newcastle, 1645; appointed lecturer
   by town council
*Oxenbridge, John   Berwick-on-Tweed, 1648
Prideaux, Richard   Lecturer at All Saints, Newcastle, 1645
Thompson, John (I)   Mitford, 1647; Bethnal with Hebburn, 1647
Trurant, Thomas   Ovingham, 1645
Ward, Ralph   Hartburn, 1655

NOTTINGHAMSHIRE

Cromwell, John   Court preacher during Protectorate, Clayworth, 1655
   (Cromwell)
Jackson, Charles   Selston, 1654
James, John   Skegby, 1652; Calverton and Woodborough, 1657; lecturer
   at Newark, 1658
Ogle, Thomas   Calverton and Woodborough, 1653; Kirton, 1655;
   Rolleston, 1657

---

[1] J. Browne, *op. cit.*   [2] F. Peck, *Desiderata Curiosa*, II, XIII, ch. 21 (1732).

*Palmer, Thomas[1] Nottingham, 1643
* *Tuke, Lemuel* Sutton in Ashfield
*Whitehurst, Richard   Askham, 1658

OXFORDSHIRE

Blower, Samuel Lecturer at Woodstock, 1657
Fenwick, John Somerton (William Sprigge[2] esq., J.P., friend of Lord Say and Sele)
Ford, Stephen Chipping Norton, 1655
*Partridge, Nathaniel Deddington, 1651
* *Rowe, John* Lecturer at Witney, 1652
* *Singleton, John* Binsey, 1659

RUTLANDSHIRE

*Ferguson, Robert   Ketton, 1657
*Fisher, James (II) Clipsham, 1629

SHROPSHIRE

*Adams, John Stoke-on-Tern, 1655
Campion, Samuel Hodnet, 1655 (Sir Henry Vernon)
* *Gilbert, Thomas* (II) Edgmond, 1649
Maurice, Henry Bromfield
* *Mayne, Zachary* St Julian's, Shrewsbury, 1658
Nevet, Rowland Stanton, 1636; Oswestry, 1647
Quarrel, Thomas Oswestry
Sadler, Richard Whixall, 1646; lecturer at Ludlow, 1652; (New England)
* *Spilsbury, John* Chetton, 1648
Thomas, Titus Aston, Edgmond

SOMERSET

*Backaller, Henry Combe St Nicholas, 1654
Baker, John Curry Mallett, 1648
* *Butler, Henry* Yeovil, 1657
*Cradock, Samuel North Cadbury, 1654; (m.d. of Charles Fleetwood)
*Elford, Thomas Trent, 1650; West Monkton, 1652
Willis, Thomas (II) Heathfield

STAFFORDSHIRE

*Adams, John Coppenhall, 1651
Badland, Thomas Willenhall, Wolverhampton, 1660
Bakewell, Thomas Rolleston, 1657

---

[1] *Congregational Hist. Soc. Trans.* IX, 31.
[2] Brother-in-law of Joshua Sprigge, a leading Independent minister. *D.N.B.* and *C.R.*

Appendix C

Bee, Henry   Hanbury, 1654
Buxton, Thomas   Tettenhall, 1655
*Hemmings, Joseph   Uttoxeter, 1648; Rolleston, 1651; chaplain to Colonel
   Pride
*Hincks, Richard   Tipton, Wolverhampton, 1652; (political radical)

Suffolk

Allen, John   Mettingham, 1643
Ames, William, jr.   Teacher at Congregational church, Wrentham (Robert
   Brewster); (educated at Harvard)
Asty, Robert   Wrentham, 1638; Stratford St Mary, 1645
Barker, Edward   Eye, 1650
*Browning, Thomas   Lecturer at Bury St Edmunds
*Chapman, Samuel   Chaplain to Lady Brooke, Yoxford
Clark, John   Lecturer, Beccles, 1643; rector, 1655
Crossman, Samuel   All Saints, Sudbury, 1647
Fenn, Stephen[1]   Southwold
Franklyn, Robert   Kirton, 1651; Westhall, 1658
*Gouge, Robert   St Helen's, Ipswich, 1654
Habergham, Samuel   Heveningham, 1650; Syleham and Wingfield, 1652
Holdborough, Thomas   Battisford, 1629
James, Thomas   Needham Market, 1650; (emigrated to New England)
*Jessey, Henry   Tutor to Gurdon family, 1629
King, James   Worlington, 1650; Debenham, 1656
King, Thomas[1]   Cove and Mutford, 1655; Wrentham, 1660
Manning, John   Walpole, 1652; Sibton with Peasenhall, 1656
Manning, Samuel   Cookley with Walpole, 1650
Manning, William   Chaplain at Landguard Fort, 1653; Middleton, 1658
Mayhew, Richard   Iken, 1657
Otty, Robert   Lecturer at Beccles
Petto, Samuel   South Elmham St Cross, 1648
Philip, John   Wrentham, 1642; (New England)
*Poynter, John   Bures St Mary, 1646
Rand, Richard   Easthorpe, 1649; Marks Tey, 1655
Smith, Zephaniah   Eyke, 1647; Chattisham, 1650; Bungay, 1656
Spatchet, Thomas   Dunwich, 1653
Spurdance, Thomas   Rushmere and Henstead?
Starke, John   Stradbroke
Stoneham, Benjamin   Oakley, 1650; Ipswich, 1651
Stoneham, Samuel[1]   Southwold
*Storer, John[1]   Lecturer at Stowmarket

[1] J. Browne, *op. cit.*

*_Taylor, Thomas_ Bury St Edmunds, 1653
*Tillinghast, John[1] Syleham
Wenbourn, John Parham
Whincop, Edmund Leiston
*_Wood, Seth_ Long Melford, 1645
Woodall, Frederick Brome, 1641, Woodbridge, 1652
Young, Thomas[1] Stowmarket

SURREY

Beerman, William[2] Chaplain to St Thomas's Hospital, Southwark, 1659
*Biscoe, John Lecturer, St George's, Southwark, 1660
*Clarkson, David Mortlake, 1656
*Cradock, Samuel Worplesdon, 1645
Cobb, Joseph Lecturer, St Thomas's Hospital, Southwark
*Cooper, William St Olave's, Southwark, 1649
*Crofts, John Ewell, 1651
Farroll, George Worplesdon, 1653 (Cromwell)
*Fisher, James (I) Fetcham, 1648
Hancock,—[2] Chaplain to St Thomas's Hospital, Southwark
*Jessey, Henry[2] Separatist congregation, Southwark, 1637; became a Baptist; lecturer at St George's, Southwark
*Maynard, John[3] Camberwell, 1646
*_Parke, Robert_ (II) Mortlake, 1654
*Pearse, Edward Richmond, 1656
*Stileman, Samuel Farnham, 1656 (Cromwell)
*_Venning, Ralph_ St Olave's, Southwark
Wavel, Richard Egham, 1658

SUSSEX

Abbot, John Midhurst, 1649; Westhampnett, 1651; New Fishbourne, 1656
Beaton, Nehemiah Little Horsted, 1661, Lurgashall, 1658; (political radical)
Crouch, John (I) Lewes
*Eston, John Pett
Garret, Richard Stedham and Heyshott, 1647
Godman, Henry Rodmell, 1652
Lover, John Hailsham, 1651

[1] J. Browne, _op. cit._
[2] On a list of Congregational ministers in and around London _c._ 1660, P.R.O.; S.P. 29–47–75.
[3] E. Cleal, _The Story of Congregationalism in Surrey._

Appendix C

*Maynard, John   Mayfield, 1624
*Parke, Robert (II)   East Lavant, 1657
Postlethwaite, Walter   Lewes, 1649
*Robotham, John   Rumboldswyke, 1647
Stonestreet, John   Lindfield, 1651
*Stoughton, William   Rumboldswyke, 1659; (New England)
Willis, John   Wool Lavington, 1654
Wilmer, Isaac   Coombes, 1658
Wilmer, Samuel   Clapham, 1651; Patching, 1654 (Cromwell)
Wilmer, Thomas   Pagham, 1654

WARWICKSHIRE

Basnet, Samuel   Town lecturer appointed by Coventry Corporation, 1653
*Collier, Abel   Nether Whitacre, 1656
*Hughes, George   Chaplain to Lord Brooke at Warwick Castle
*Machin, John   Lecturer at Atherstone
*Partridge, Nathaniel   Chaplain to Charles Fleetwood, 1670; Burton
    Dassett, 1647
Walden, Gilbert   Leamington Hastings, 1652
*Wright, James   Wootton Wawen, 1661

WESTMORLAND

*Marsden, Jeremiah   Lecturer at Kendal, 1659

WILTSHIRE

*Byefield, Adoniram[1]   Collingbourne Ducis
Baylie, Thomas   Mildenhall, 1647 (Fifth Monarchist?)
Chauncey, Isaac   Woodborough, 1656 (Cromwell); (educated in New
    England)
Crouch, John (II)   Alderbury, 1656
*Eyre, William   Compton Bassett, 1641; Odstock, 1645; Salisbury, 1647
Hughes, William   Bromham, 1639; St Mary's, Marlborough, 1649
Rashley, Thomas?   Barford St Martin and Salisbury, 1652; (New England)
*Troughton, William   St Martin's, Salisbury, 1653
*Wills, Obadiah   Alton Barnes, 1656
Woodbridge, John   Barford St Martin, 1650; (New England)

WORCESTERSHIRE

Fincher, Richard   All Saints and St Nicholas, Worcester, 1652
*Hincks, Richard   Pensax, 1657; (political radical)
Jordon, Timothy   Great Comberton, 1654; Eckington, 1656; (political
    radical)

[1] D.N.B.

149

Juice, Thomas   St Martin's, Worcester, 1650
Moor, Simon   St Michael's, Worcester, and Cathedral preacher, 1647;
   (political radical)
Oasland, Henry   Bewdley, 1650
*Spilsbury, John   Bromsgrove, 1654
*Sumptner, Charles   Army Chaplain; Staunton, 1653
Westmacot, William   Cropthorne, 1648 (Cromwell)

YORKSHIRE

Bloom, Matthew   Attercliffe, Sheffield, 1657 (paid by Corporation)
Bowles, Edward   Preacher at York Minster, 1646; chaplain in Army;
   (friend of Monk)
Canne, John[1]   Hull, 1650
Coore, Richard   Heptonstall, 1645; Halifax, 1650; Tong, Birstall, 1650;
   (Antinomian)
Fisher, James (II)   Sheffield, 1648
Gunter, John   Bedale
Holdsworth, Josiah   Sutton-upon-Derwent, 1657
Izott, John   Nun Monkton, 1656 (son of John, elder in Congregational
   church, Woodkirk, Yorks.)
Jackson, John   Cantley and Austerfield, 1650
Jackson, Nathaniel   Barwick in Elmet, 1650
*Jessey, Henry   Aughton, 1633
*Luddington, Robert   Hull, 1643; Sculcoates, 1650; Skidby, 1657
*Marsden, Gamaliel   St Anne's, Halifax, 1660
*Marsden, Jeremiah   Thornton, Bradford, 1650; Halifax, 1651; chaplain
   at Hull, 1659; East Ardsley, 1662
*Marshall, Christopher   Woodkirk, 1650; (emigrated to New England)
Milner, Jeremiah   Rothwell, 1659
Nesse, Christopher   South Cliff, Cottingham, 1651; lecturer at Leeds, 1656
*Nye, Philip   Hull, 1640
*Oxenbridge, John   Beverley and Hull, 1644
Richardson, Christopher   Kirkheaton, 1648
Root, Henry   Sowerby Bridge, Halifax, 1661
*Shawe, John   Rotherham, 1639; Darfield, 1646; Hull, 1651
*Smallwood, Thomas   Scammonden, 1642; Woodkirk, 1653; Batley,
   1654
Taylor, Richard   Chaplain to Sir Edward Rhodes, Great Houghton,
   Darfield
*Town, Robert   Haworth, 1650; (Antinomian)

[1] D.N.B.

Appendix C

*Tricket, Mark   Laughton, 1657; Adlingfleet, 1660
*Whitehurst, Richard   Laughton, 1659
*Winter, Samuel   Ousebridge, 1641; Cottingham, 1643

IRELAND

*Amyraut, Paul
*Marsden, Gamaliel   Trinity College, Dublin, 1654
*Marsden, Jeremiah
Marsden, Josiah   Trinity College, Dublin, 1658
*Mather, Samuel   Dublin, 1655
*Owen, John   Chaplain to Cromwell
*Partridge, Nathaniel   1653
*Peters, Hugh   Army Chaplain
*Sumptner, Charles   Army Chaplain
* Wale,—[1]
*Winter, Samuel   Trinity College, Dublin, 1651
*Wood, Robert

UNIVERSITY POSITIONS

Oxford

Allen, James   Fellow of New College, 1649–60
Angier, Samuel   Student of Christ Church
*Avery, Richard   Magdalen
Button, Ralph   Canon of Christ Church
Charnock, Stephen   New Inn Hall; (seems to have been in close contact with Protectorate government)
Cole, Thomas   St Mary's Hall, 1656
du Moulin, Lewis   Professor of Ancient History, 1646
*Gale, Theophilus   Fellow of Magdalen
Hickman, Henry   Magdalen; (very liberal)
Howell, Francis   Principal of Jesus College, 1657
Johnson, Francis   Chaplain to Cromwell; Master of University College
*Lee, Samuel   Wadham, 1648
*Marshall, Walter   New College, 1648
*Mather, Samuel   Magdalen, 1653; (educated in New England)
*Owen, John   Dean of Christ Church
Owen, Thankful   St John's, 1650
*Palmer, Anthony   Balliol, 1640
Porter, George   Magdalen and Christ Church
*Poynter, John   Christ Church (Cromwell)
Risley, Thomas   Pembroke

[1] F. Peck, *op. cit.*

Rogers, Christopher   New Inn Hall; (political radical)
*Singleton, John   Christ Church
*Spilsbury, John   Magdalen
*Sprigge, Joshua[1]   All Souls, 1649
Sprigge, William[1]   Lincoln College; (brother of Joshua Sprigge)
*Stoughton, William   New College
Thompson, John (II)   Christ Church
*Wills, Obadiah   New College
*Wood, Robert   Lincoln College, 1649

Cambridge

*Chapman, Samuel   Corpus Christi
*Clarkson, David   Clare
*Corbyn, Samuel   Trinity, 1655
Day, James   Emmanuel
Ekins, Robert   Trinity, 1655
Fairclough, Samuel   Caius, 1651
Holcroft, Francis   Fellow of Clare
Hutchinson, Joseph   Trinity, 1659
Lock, Thomas   Trinity, 1657
*Loeffs, Isaac   Peterhouse, 1645
Moore, Thomas   Magdalene; (very liberal theology)
Oddy, Joseph   Trinity, 1658
Plumstead, Augustine   Trinity
*Simpson, Sidrach[1]   Pembroke Hall, 1650

OTHER APPOINTMENTS

*Avery, Richard   Chaplain to Richard Cromwell's wife
*Cromwell, John   Court preacher during Protectorate
*Goodwin, Thomas   Minister in attendance at Whitehall, 1649; lay preacher, 1645; chaplain of Eton, 1654–60; (pro-Cromwell)
*Lockyer, Nicholas   Preacher at Windsor Castle, 1649; sent to Scotland by Council, 1651; preacher at Whitehall, 1653; Provost of Eton, 1658
*Mead, Matthew   Preacher to Council at Whitehall
*Oxenbridge, John   Eton
*Peters, Hugh[1]   Army chaplain and Government Agent; chaplain at Whitehall; (Holland and New England)
*Sprigge, Joshua[1]   Possibly chaplain to Fairfax
White, Jeremiah   Chaplain to Cromwell; (lived at St Albans 1648)

[1] *D.N.B.*

Appendix C

Carter, William[1]   Early leading Independent
Faldo, John   Not beneficed
Mence, Francis   C.R.
Powell, Vavasor[2]   Wales
Wright, John[3]   Woodborough, Notts. or Wilts.

These ministers returned from New England, but I have no more information about them:[4] Richard Blinam, Charles Chauncey, Downing, John Hoadley, J. Hobart, John Hooke, William Knight, John Leverett, M. Matthews, John Millard, Robert Peck, Josiah Swinebrook, Thomas Thompson, Fitzjohn Winthrop.

[1] B. Hanbury, *Historical Memorials of the Independents*, II, 494.
[2] F. Peck, *op. cit.* and *D.N.B.*   [3] F. Peck, *op. cit.*
[4] W. L. Sachse, 'The Migration of New Englanders to America', *American Historical Review*, LIII, 264.

SELECT BIBLIOGRAPHY

MANUSCRIPTS

Diary of Sir James Harrington, British Museum Additional MSS. 10,114.
Members of John Owen's Congregation, 1659. British Museum Lansdowne MSS. folios 823-251. March 1659.
Purchasers of Bishops' Lands, Bodleian Library, Rawlinson MSS. B. 239.
A List of Congregational Ministers Petitioning Charles II. P.R.O., S.P. 29-1-28.
Congregational Ministers in and around London, 1660. P.R.O., S.P. 29-47-75.
Notes on Members of the Long Parliament, by W. D. Pink. John Rylands Library, Manchester.
Notes on Members of the Long Parliament, by C. V. Wedgwood. Institute of Historical Research, London.

CONTEMPORARY MEMOIRS, PAPERS AND COLLECTIONS OF DOCUMENTS

A Secret Negotiation, Camden Society Miscellany (1883).
Baillie, Robert, A Dissuasive from the Errors of the Time (1645).
—— Letters and Journal, ed. D. Laing, 3 vols. (Edinburgh, 1841).
Barnes, Ambrose, Memoirs, ed. W. H. D. Longstaffe, Surtees Society (1867).
Bastwick, John, Independency not God's Ordinance (1645).
Baxter, Richard, Reliquae Baxterianae (1896).
Brooke, Robert Greville, Lord, A Discourse opening the Nature of that Episcopacy (1642).
Burton, Thomas, Diary of Thomas Burton Esquire, ed. J. T. Rutt, 4 vols. (1828).
Calamy, Edmund, Account of the Ministers...Ejected or Silenced (1713).
—— Continuation of the Account (1727).
Clarendon, Edward Hyde, Earl of, History of the Rebellion, 7 vols. (Oxford, 1849).
Coleman, T., Hopes Deferred and Dashed (1645).
Cotton, John, Keys of the Kingdom of Heaven (1644).
—— The Ways of the Churches of Christ in New England (1645).
Cromwell, Oliver, Writings and Speeches, ed. W. C. Abbott, 4 vols. (Harvard, 1937-47).
Edwards, Thomas, Gangraena (1646).
Hanbury, Benjamin, Historical Memorials relating to the Independents, 3 vols. (1839-44).

Select Bibliography

Harrington, James, *Noah's Dove* (1645).

Harris, John, *The Royal Quarrel* (1647).

Holles, Denzil, Lord, 'Memoirs' reprinted in *Select Tracts*, ed. Francis Maseres, 2 vols. (1815).

Hutchinson, Lucy, *Memoirs of the Life of Colonel Hutchinson*, Everyman Edition (1913).

Independency Stript and Whipt (1648).

Letter of an Independent to Mr Glyn (1645).

Ludlow, Edmund, *Memoirs*, ed. C. H. Firth, 2 vols. (Oxford, 1894).

Mercurius Aulicus (2 April 1643).

Original Letters and Papers of State addressed to Oliver Cromwell, ed. J. Nicholls (1743).

Palmer, S., *The Nonconformist's Memorial*; 2nd ed. 3 vols. (1802).

Peck, Francis, *Desiderata Curiosa*, 2 vols. (1732).

Peter, Hugh, *Good Work for a Good Magistrate* (1651).

Philalattes, Salem, *The Moderate Independent Proposing a Word in Season to the Gathered Churches* (1660).

Rushworth, John, *Historical Collections*, 7 vols. (1659–1701).

The Independent Military Entertainment (1645).

The Reconciler earnestly endeavouring to unite in sincere affection the Presbyters and their Dissenting Brethren (1646).

Thornton, Alice, *Autobiography*, Surtees Society (1875).

Vicars, John, *The Picture of Independency Carefully yet Lovingly Delineated* (1645).

Walker, Clement, *The History of Independency* (1660).

Whitelocke, Bulstrode, *Memorials of the English Affairs*, 4 vols. (Oxford, 1863).

Woodhouse, A. S. P., *Puritanism and Liberty* (1938).

LATER WORKS

The place of publication is London, unless otherwise indicated.

Ashley, M. P., *Cromwell's Generals* (1954).

Bate, F., *The Declaration of Indulgence* (1908).

Brosley, Ira, *The Ministers of the Abbey Church* (1911).

Browne, J., *History of Congregationalism...in Norfolk and Suffolk* (1877).

Browne, L. F., *The Political Activities of the Baptists and Fifth Monarchy Men* (1912).

Broxap, E., *The Great Civil War in Lancashire* (Manchester, 1910).

Brunton, D. and Pennington, D. H., *Members of the Long Parliament* (1954).

Burrage, C., *The Early English Dissenters*, 2 vols. (Cambridge, 1912).

Cleal, E. E., *The Story of Congregationalism in Surrey* (1905).

The Independents in the Civil War

Coate, M., *Cornwall in the Great Civil War* (Oxford, 1933).

Congregational Historical Society Transactions, vols. 6, 7, 9, 13, 14.

Densham, W. and Ogle, J., *The Story of the Congregational Churches of Dorset* (Bournemouth, 1899).

Halley, R., *Lancashire, its Puritanism and Nonconformity*, 2 vols. (Manchester, 1869).

Harte, W. J., 'Puritanism in Devonshire', *Devonshire Association Transactions* (1937).

Hexter, J. H., 'The Problem of the Presbyterian Independents', *American Historical Review* (1938).

—— *The Reign of King Pym* (Harvard, 1941).

Jordan, W. K., *The Development of Religious Toleration in England*, 4 vols. (1932–40).

—— *Men of Substance* (Chicago, 1942).

Keeler, M. F., *The Long Parliament 1640–1641* (Philadelphia, 1954).

Matthews, A. G., *Calamy Revised* (Oxford, 1934).

—— *The Congregational Churches of Staffordshire* (1924).

Nobbs, D., 'Philip Nye on Church and State', *Cambridge Historical Journal* (1935).

Nuttall, G. F., 'Congregational Commonwealth Incumbents', *Congregational Historical Society Transactions* (1943).

—— *The Holy Spirit in Puritan Faith and Experience* (Oxford, 1946).

—— *Visible Saints—The Congregational Way 1640–1660* (Oxford, 1957).

Sasche, W. L., 'The Migration of New Englanders to England', *American Historical Review* (1955).

Saunders, H. F., 'Nottinghamshire Independency', *Congregational Historical Society Transactions* (1935).

Shaw, W. A., *History of the English Church during the Civil Wars...1640–60* (1900).

Sibree, J. and Caston, M., *Independency in Warwickshire* (Coventry, 1855).

Thomas-Sanford, C., *Sussex in the Great Civil War* (1910).

Trevor-Roper, H. R., 'The Gentry 1540–1640', *Economic History Review*, Supplement (1953).

Urwick, W., *Nonconformity in Hertfordshire* (1884).

Wharton, E. R., *The Whartons of Wharton Hall* (Oxford, 1898).

Wood, A. C., *Nottinghamshire in the Civil War* (Oxford, 1937).